families with faith

Survival skills for Christian parents

Richard Patterson

FAMILIES WITH FAITH by Richard Patterson

Scripture Union, 207–209 Queensway, Bletchley, MK2 2EB, UK
email: info@scriptureunion.org.uk
www.scriptureunion.org.uk

Scripture Union USA: PO Box 987 #1, Valley Forge, PA 19482
Email: info@scriptureunion.org
www.scriptureunion.org

Scripture Union Australia: Locked Bag 2, Central Coast Business Centre, NSW 2252
www.su.org.au

ISBN 978 184427 247 1

First published in Great Britain by Scripture Union 2007. Some of the content was previously released in an earlier US edition as *It's the little things that count*.

© Richard Patterson

Scripture quotations, unless otherwise indicated, are taken from the HOLY BIBLE, NEW INTERNATIONAL VERSION (NIV), copyright © 1973, 1978, 1984 by International Bible Society. Used by permission of Hodder & Stoughton Ltd.

British Library Cataloguing-in-Publication data: a catalogue record for this book is available from the British Library.

Cover design by David Lund Design, Milton Keynes.
Internal page design by Creative Pages: creativepages.co.uk
Printed and bound by Bookmarque, Croydon.

Scripture Union is an international Christian charity working with churches in more than 130 countries providing resources to bring the good news about Jesus Christ to children, young people and families – and to encourage them to develop spiritually through the Bible and prayer. As well as a network of volunteers, staff and associates who run holidays, church-based events and school Christian groups, Scripture Union produces a wide range of publications and supports those who use their resources through training programmes.

About the author

Rich Patterson has been married for 35 years, and he and his wife Sara are the parents of two grown sons. Before assuming his present position in the editorial department of Scripture Union USA, Rich served for 15 years as their Children and Family Ministries Specialist. During that time, he spoke to many parents at conferences all over the eastern United States. He has written four books and numerous magazine articles on parenting and family life and is frequently quoted in newspaper articles.

Rich's hobbies include reading and choral singing. And he is a great fan of the BBC science fiction series *Dr Who*! During his college years, he studied for a year at the London School of Economics and has since visited the UK twice. He says he is anxious to return, especially to travel in Scotland. Rich is an ordained minister in the Presbyterian Church, USA.

To my wife Sara and my sons Jeremy and Zachary

*I've learned much and received much more
from being a family with them*

CONTENTS

Foreword

Train a child in the way he should go, and when he is old he will not turn from it.
Proverbs 22:6

Nic and Sue Cooper

UK Premier Christian Radio's 'Married Couple of the Year 2006'

BEING A twenty-first century parent presents many challenges. So many of us live permanently in the fast lane; inevitably at some point we'll arrive at hazards we're unable to negotiate as well as we'd like. Life's journey sometimes involves us in some serious problems and pressures.

As a couple, we've already encountered many challenges in parenting, not least helping our two boys make good decisions about TV and what to do about football matches on Sundays. Our aim is for open communication with Christian and Matthew at all times, and that includes letting them know when we're struggling and showing them how we bring our difficulties to God. We want to live in ways that encourage our boys, now teenagers, in their own relationship with God. We realise there's no point in them living off our faith; if they try to do that, they'll fall at the first hurdle.

Families with Faith is a book that provides valuable insights into how parents can invest – or re-invest – time into their family life. There's excellent advice on making good choices about your work/home life balance, on family mealtimes, children's bedtimes and discipline. We enjoyed the tips about how as a married couple we can show more love to each other. And we loved the chapter on praying for your children – something we've always worked at with our two boys. The questions at the end of each chapter are great because they help to recap the material and give you something to work on.

Author Richard Patterson intertwines practical guidelines with biblical principles. He emphasises that 'the most success is enjoyed by families whose life together is undergirded by a commitment to live by the principles of faith, to follow the path in life set out for them by Jesus Christ'. We totally agree that this must be the foundation that every believing parent builds their family life on if we want to reap the full blessing that God is longing to give us.

This is a book we wholeheartedly recommend to parents and would-be parents, and to anyone working in their communities to encourage godly parenting.

Introduction: Families surviving and thriving

IT'S TOUGH being a family today. Everyone is so busy; everything is so rushed. Our lives are all stuck in 'fast forward'. 'Hyper-parents' run their children from one activity to the next. Work commitments steal both time and energy from our family life. Marriages starve for lack of time and space for spouses to nurture and grow their love. Sometimes, it seems everything is working against having a happy, successful family! It's just no fun anymore.

That's the bad news. The good news is that families – including *your* family – can survive the challenges and overcome the obstacles they face. And not just survive, but thrive! I know it's possible. I've seen it.

I've been a parent for over 30 years. During most of that time, I've been involved in working with parents, listening to them share their ups and downs, and watching them quietly go about the business of building families that survive and thrive in the midst of incredible stress and powerful threats. I've seen it in families of all kinds: single-parent families, two-parent families, and step- and blended families too.

But families that survive in today's family-hostile culture don't do it by accident. My experience is that the most success is enjoyed by families whose life together is undergirded by a commitment to live by the principles of faith, to follow the path in life set out for them by Jesus Christ. And they've learned to live by **six simple survival skills** that enable them to thrive while other families are 'going under'. In the pages that follow, we'll explore those survival skills together and look at the practical, everyday ways they help families survive – and thrive!

Facing up to the situation

But first, let's look briefly at just what families today are up against. Some understanding of that will better equip us to see how to win the battle for survival!

There are three major and closely related pressures threatening families today, all related to time. There's
- the **family time famine** that robs families of time to enjoy each other and to build strong, rewarding relationships;
- the **job-first culture** that robs parents of time and energy to invest in their families;
- the **fragility of marriages**, which often are strained because husbands and wives struggle to find time and energy to invest in nurturing their relationship.

Every family feels, or has felt, one – if not all – of these pressures. How your family handles them is crucial to surviving and thriving as a family with faith.

Mastering our time

Because time pressures are at the core of many of the obstacles families face today, the first survival skill we'll discuss is that of mastering the family's time: getting control of out-of-control family schedules. Chapter 1 offers ways – large and small – in which ordinary families can survive the 'time crunch', stay connected and grow together.

What were once normal family activities – family meals, visits to relatives, weekend outings, time to talk and have fun together – are becoming optional, not experiences that children are entitled to expect as members of a family. Families of faith recognise the need to step back from the rat race regularly to be physically and spiritually renewed. So in chapter 2 we'll look at the perhaps frightening, perhaps revolutionary, practice of observing a 'family Sabbath'. There may be some surprises there, but I think you'll find that chapter especially intriguing.

The UK's 'long hours culture' forces every family every day to engage in a precarious juggling act, balancing work and family life. How does yours cope? We'll consider that in chapter 3.

Many family 'flavours'

Families come in many varieties today: two-parent, lone- or single-parent, step-families, blended families and others! Each kind of family has its own challenges and rewards.

In chapter 4 we'll examine some of the challenges that married couples face and, more importantly, we'll see some practical, everyday ways to build and maintain strong and rewarding marriages. Isn't that what every married couple wants?

In chapter 5 we'll see how single-parent families and blended families successfully overcome the major obstacles they face. They may not be what some people think of as traditional families but I know that they can be just as strong and rewarding as any other family. By following some simple, basic guidelines they too can survive and thrive.

Building the family faith

Underneath everything that is said in the pages that follow is the assumption that the strongest, most rewarding families – the families most able to survive in a family-hostile culture – are families with faith who trust in God and his divine son, Jesus Christ. But faith isn't inherited like hair colour or personality. It must be taught and nurtured in each generation. So, in chapter 6, we'll examine some proven principles for passing on our faith to our children – right in the midst of busy, messy everyday family life. They're time-tested and parent-approved over many generations!

One of the most potent tools God has given parents for nurturing faith in their families is prayer, so in chapter 7 I'll share some ways and occasions parents can effectively pray for their children. It's a key survival skill!

Let's celebrate!

Sometimes the pressures and responsibilities of daily family life seem relentless. How do you survive the inevitable 'dark days' and stresses of family life? My answer is: celebrate – any time and every time you can! In chapter 8 we'll explore the joys and rewards of family rituals and traditions, big and small. You may be surprised how even modest celebrations create wonderful memories and enable families to enjoy ordinary family life in quite extraordinary ways. After all, why shouldn't family life be fun, at least once in a while? Family fun is seriously important to family health and survival, and it needn't be time-consuming or expensive. There'll be plenty of examples awaiting you in chapter 9.

> For our struggle is not against flesh and blood, but against the rulers, against the authorities, against the powers of this dark world…
> *Ephesians 6:12*

Thinking positive about discipline

One of the least appealing aspects of family life is establishing and maintaining discipline. From the perspective of us parents, it's often a necessary evil. After all, no family can survive and thrive without good discipline. But discipline is so much more than 'keeping the kids under control'. It's really about *discipling* our children. Discipline as discipling is a vital survival skill for all families of faith, so in chapter 10 we'll look at some key principles of good discipline and the practical ways to apply them.

Churches and families together

Families of faith celebrate, nourish and express their faith in worship and service through their local church, often giving much. But what can their church give them in return? How can local churches help families survive the stresses and pressures they face? That's the focus of chapter 11. I'll share some imaginative ways in which churches of all denominations and sizes are supporting families, both in their congregations and in their surrounding neighbourhoods.

Join me for the journey

You'll find it helpful to pause at the end of each section to ask yourself the questions listed. Even better, invite a small group of people (maybe four to eight others) who are struggling with some of the same issues and work through the material together. You could commit to tackling one chapter a week, and get together informally over coffee and snacks to chat about the content and look at the questions together. Alternatively, talk to your church leader about using the book within an existing small group programme. There's real strength in tackling big issues with other people.

Now it's time to begin our journey. Join me as we walk together through the mysterious, frustrating, wild and wonderful world of daily family life. So many families are sinking under the weight of the pressures they face today. But I believe your family can do better – much better. They can not only survive – but thrive!

If you are a church leader, church-based group or concerned individual, this book could be invaluable as the basis for a parenting course in your community. For free downloadable advice on how to do that, go to www.scriptureunion.org.uk/families

SURVIVAL SKILL 1

Mastering the family's time

1 Surviving the time crunch and staying connected

ONE OF THE biggest sources of stress on families today is the **family time famine**: not enough time spent together to survive and thrive as a family. Yet our own intuition backs up what experts say: happy, healthy families spend generous quantities of quality time with each other. After a shared commitment to Christ, spending time together is perhaps the most crucial element in making families strong and happy.

Practically every survey of families reveals lack of time to be together as one of the top sources of family stress. Yet family unity, belonging and warmth must be nurtured and grown over time, just as a lovely garden grows over the seasons in the hands of a caring, diligent gardener. Without quality time together, all aspects of family life, including the spiritual, are undermined.

> There is a time for everything, and a season for every activity under heaven.
> *Ecclesiastes 3:1*

Making the most of family life every day

In chapter 3 we'll look at why families are time-starved. But let's start by accepting the situation and think about how to tackle it.

The cliché holds true: there are only 24 hours in each day. To survive and thrive in a time-starved world, strong families don't try just to find *more* time for their families, they make the *most* of the time they already have. The key survival skill is to identify and maximise the opportunities – using the time we already spend with our family in a way that has the greatest impact for family health. Secondly, it means identifing the key activities – large and small – that mean the most to family life and investing our limited time in them to stay strong and connected as a family. It's all about investing our time where it will yield the greatest rewards for our family. The key is to start with what we're already doing.

Let's begin by looking at four key areas of family life: bedtime, homework time, family meals and weekends. We'll also look at strategies involving our use of the phone and family car trips. Let's look at bedtime first.

Being there at bedtime

When Dickens described life in Revolutionary France as 'the best of times … the worst of times', he could have been describing bedtime in any home with young children. Getting two or three (or more!) young children bathed, into their pajamas, through their stories and prayers and (finally) into bed can require all the discipline and energy of running a marathon.

Cleaning and scrubbing can wait 'til tomorrow;
For babies grow up, we've learned to our sorrow.
So quiet down, cobwebs, dust, go to sleep;
I'm rocking my baby – and babies don't keep.
Anon

But a young child's bedtime can also be a very special time, when he or she snuggles up on mum or dad's lap to read a story and say their bedtime prayers. At its best, bedtime is a daily ritual that can reaffirm for our children our great love for them, and can reassure them about how special they are to us and to the God whose love and care we represent.

The problem is that this special ritual takes time. All shapes and sizes of families struggle to find those few precious moments to spend with each child at the end of the day. How can they do it?

Two-parent families can rotate bedtime responsibilities on

any given night so that over the course of a week each parent puts the children to bed at least a couple of times. The rotation can be planned and adjusted to compensate for when one parent has to be away at bedtime. For some families – especially single parents – separate bedtimes, even 15 minutes apart, may be the answer. Those few minutes where the parent can focus on each child individually provide a daily answer to a young child's often felt but seldom voiced question: 'Am I really someone special in this family?'

And bedtime isn't just for mothers. In fact, dads are even more essential at bedtime if they tend to be less physically present in the home. Dad's presence at bedtime assures the children of the love and dependable care of *both* parents and of the reality and stability of the family unit. Lone parents who make it a priority to be there for *most* bedtimes send their children the same important message.

Missing your child's bedtime now and then is no cause for guilt. But what if you simply can't be there at bedtime with any regularity at all?

Perhaps your situation is like that of a single mum I know who works nights. Even though she sees her son after school and before she goes to work, she uses her coffee break to call him around bedtime. It's a 'check-in' and 'good night' call all in one. In about ten minutes, she can ask if he's finished his homework, and listen as he brings her up to date on his life since the school day ended. Then she wishes him good night. In a real sense, her son knows she is 'there' at bedtime and has affirmed her care for him, even though she must be at work and it's the childminder that's physically there.

Routine or ritual?

Bedtime can easily become just another daily routine chore. But it can be so much more than that. Bedtime can be a daily ritual filled with all the meaning, symbolism, and emotional and spiritual power of other family rituals such as weddings, birthday parties or decorating the Christmas tree. Not surprisingly, children find great spiritual and emotional nurture in the bedtime ritual. When the lights go out, the parent leaves and the door is closed, a young child can be very frightened. The predictability and warmth of bedtime deepens a young child's faith that their parents can be counted on to be there for them all through the long night and once again in the morning. This is the beginning of their understanding of the totally dependable, unceasing love and care of God. God and their parents are with them. Of what in life need they be afraid?

God's people have always seen bedtime as an important family ritual. In Deuteronomy 6, where Moses is instructing the Israelites in the spiritual nurture of their children, he specifically mentions bedtime ('… when you lie down …' 6:7). Israelite parents were to use that time to remind their children of God's blessings during the day and his work in the past (through a Bible story), all expressed with a prayer of thanks.

Bedtime may only require a few minutes, especially as children get older. But potentially it is quality time. Be there as often as you can, and make the most of it!

Making light work of homework

Mention homework to just about any school-age child and their reaction is likely to be either a pained look or a loud groan. And exchanges of, 'Get that homework done this minute,' and 'But it's not fair,' don't exactly make for warm family feelings! But since you're probably going to spend some time helping your children with their homework anyway, why not try to spend this time together as positively as possible?

The key to success here is perspective. Homework time is an opportunity for you and your child to work together towards a common goal: homework completed well and progress made towards good grades. As long as you both can be patient with each other and the atmosphere is reasonably pleasant, it *can* work. Common projects bind people together and reinforce their sense of family ties – even projects such as homework.

A BBC survey found that parents spend on average six hours a week helping their children with homework. In addition to the benefits that result to the children and the family, their report tells parents that, 'You'll get to know your child's particular strengths and difficulties and you will also find out what she's studying. Your child's school will also gain by having motivated pupils and well-informed parents who are fully involved with their child's education.' Suggested guidelines for the time a child spends on homework are:

Age 5-7 – 1 hour per week

Age 8,9 – 1.5 hours per week

Age 10,11 – 30 minutes a day

Age 12,13 – 45–90 minutes a day

Age 14 – 1–2 hours a day

Age 15,16 – 1.5–2.5 hours a day

Begin by communicating your expectations clearly to your children. This involves such things as what time to start homework and the fact that you may review its quality at any time on any night. You can be both positive and proactive by beginning this way: 'I want you to do well. You'll be proud of yourself for your accomplishments. If you have problems, we can probably work them out together.' (In my case, maths was specifically excluded!) The parent is proactive: 'I can't do your homework for you but I'll be available to help in any way I can.'

Experts agree that the children who are most successful in school are the ones whose parents show significant interest in their studies. Helping with homework underscores our interest in and our commitment to the success of our children. Help offered in a positive, affirming, confidence-building way ('Let's see if we can work this out together') is really a very practical demonstration of love.

Family mealtimes – an endangered species?

In my family our Thanksgiving Day celebration has always been an experience to be greatly anticipated. For over 25 years, my wife and I and our kids have joined with my parents and siblings, numerous aunts and uncles and their children and spouses, not to mention assorted friends, for Thanksgiving dinner. There are usually at least 25 of us gathered at my uncle's house on the edge of my brothers' dairy farm in northern New York state.

Scripture Union's Family Activity Organiser
See page 206 for details.

It is a real gathering of the clan for the Pattersons – a meaningful annual reminder of our roots, of those with whom we share a common heritage and of how much we all have to be thankful for. It is just about the only time of the year we know we'll all see each other and be able to catch up on the life of the wider Patterson family. Perhaps Christmas or New Year is like that for your family?

In a smaller but no less real sense, that's what a daily family mealtime offers families. A daily meal together, usually in the evening, is the one time each day when parents and children are assured of uninterrupted time with each other, to keep in touch emotionally as well as physically.

A 1977 Demos Report 'Family Learning' said that 'children who participate in family mealtime discussions develop the highest aptitude for reading and vocabulary … mealtime conversations use ten times more sophisticated words than other situations, including school lessons and playtimes.'

But, faced with an over-full family calendar and increasingly complex and demanding work schedules, fewer families in both the UK and the US eat an evening meal together. The decline of this important daily appointment represents a significant loss, especially for children. Talking around the table has been replaced as people sit in front of the TV, chewing silently on a microwave dinner from a tray. Gone is the sharing of the events of daily life, the venting of frustrations, the hatching of plans.

Important for teens

Experts in adolescent development stress that the daily investment in family mealtime pays big dividends, especially during the teen years. Studies consistently find that in families where the parents eat the evening meal with their teens at least five nights each week, teens are less likely to smoke, take drugs, be depressed or get in trouble with the law. They are more likely to do well in school and enjoy a happy circle of friends than teens whose parents eat with them three evenings a week or less. Yet only about a quarter of teens eat with their parents each evening. Surprisingly, most teens surveyed – far from wanting to get away from their parents – wished they could share a meal with them more often.

Family mealtimes obviously offer more than just food for the body. They feed our spirits, also. As we give thanks together for our food, touch base about our day and share the high and low points, we remember and celebrate the goodness of God and God's care for us.

Mealtimes are our oldest rituals,' says a *Guardian* newspaper report by Felipe Fernández-Armesto, author of *Food: a History*. Particularly attacking new work patterns, fast food and the microwave, Fernández-Armesto writes, 'The little links which bind households together are forged at the table. The stability of our home probably depends more on regular mealtimes than on sexual fidelity or filial piety. Now it is in danger. Food is being desocialised... The loneliness of the fast-food eater is uncivilising... Lunch has disappeared in favour of daytime grazing. People ... snack in the streets, trailing litter ... Latchkey kids come home alone and fall ravenously on instantly infused pot noodles ... '

A family sacrament

To explain to their children the difference between heaven and hell, Koreans tell a wonderful story which emphasises how rich an experience the family mealtime can be.

The story tells how the people in hell sit at large tables beautifully spread with all kinds of fine, delicious food. Their punishment is that they are eternally unable to eat and enjoy the food because their chopsticks are seven feet long (so their arms aren't long enough to feed themselves).

In heaven, the tables of delicious food and the seven-foot chopsticks are identical – but the people *do* enjoy the marvellous feast. Their joy is evident. Why? They feed each other! Family mealtime reminds us that the greatest joys in life are ones that come from serving and feeding those we love the most.

A regular family mealtime is, in a real sense, a family sacrament. It feeds our bodies, emotions and spirits, and we can celebrate in this way every day. Of course, unavoidable diary clashes will arise. Don't feel guilty. But regular or deliberately-scheduled infringements on the family meal-time (such as work appointments) are unacceptable. Let the phone ring or assure the caller that you'll call back after the meal. Be prepared to plan your mealtimes flexibly to accommodate different schedules. Keep a family organiser pinned up in the kitchen and hallway, and expect everyone to register their commitments. But consider challenging the timing of sports games, music practices or even church activities if they are at times which obviously conflict with most families' evening mealtimes. If you absolutely can't make it home for the evening meal most weeknights, try to have breakfast together and make weekend meals a priority. One busy doctor I know who's always home late gathers his family together for a snack or dessert and some time to talk on his arrival. He understands that observing a family meatime is one very important survival skill for strong families.

Weekends were made for families

A generation ago, weekends were more relaxed times for families. In recent years that has changed dramatically. The British organisation *Keep Time for Children* exists entirely to 'promote the importance of family time at weekends, particularly for families with school age children'. It notes that 'the growth of the 24/7 culture and particularly the rise of weekend working has meant that many children of school age don't see their parents nearly as much as they should.'

And, if we aren't working, our weekends are often spent driving our children to sports practices or to shop or meet their friends. Any time left over after our chauffeur duties is eaten up by a seemingly inexhaustible list of our own errands!

The problem with weekends is that I always seem to have a long list of chores and urgent projects which have been waiting all week for my attention. Perhaps that happens to you too. So how do I make time for my children?

Often it's possible to include at least one of your children in your errands and chores. For quite a number of years we lived where there was an ice cream shop just two doors down from the hardware store. So, if I needed to go to the store on Saturday, I would take the boys along and stop off for an ice cream treat!

For a time, I was working late three nights each week, so we developed a favourite Saturday morning ritual. While Mum slept in, the boys and I would go out for an early breakfast at a local fast food restaurant. The three of us looked forward to it and when we got back to the house around 9am there was still plenty of time left for my jobs. If you're counting the pennies, maybe you could make a picnic breakfast and take it out to eat.

One family I know schedules one Saturday morning each month for family outings and fun activities. The date is marked on the family calendar well in advance. Because it's on their calendar, if other obligations come up, they can truthfully say, 'I already have an appointment then'.

Staying available and connected

I had an appointment with the chief executive officer of a large foundation. Before our conversation hardly got past the 'hello' stage, he took a phone call. Soon it became obvious he was talking to his son. The call went on for nearly ten minutes and I began to get a little frustrated. I had prepared long and hard for this appointment. I felt I needed – and deserved – his full attention. Couldn't he talk to his son at home after work?

When the call was over, he explained, 'My son is away at college. It's his first year. I told him that anytime he needs to talk to me, for any reason, just to call. I'll be available. My secretary knows to always put him through to me.'

This man's availability to talk at any time during the work day communicated to his son that 'no one or nothing is more important to me than you are. If you need me, just call. I'm available.'

It's true that we can't always be with our children when either they or we would wish it. But, as a psychologist at a major American university put it, 'the cell phone is the saviour here'. Many parents and children use them (along with email and texting) to keep in touch, even when they aren't physically together. These tools help us be available to our children when they need us.

The after-school connection

One increasingly popular way the phone keeps parents in touch with their children is during that after-school period. Many working parents fight a daily anxiety attack that afflicts them about ten minutes after their children are supposed to have arrived home from school.

'I just need to know they are home', said one working mother of an 11- and a 12-year-old.

'I just look at the clock and by 3:10 I start calling and getting really nervous.'

A call from her children with a simple, 'Hi, Mum, we're home,' is all she needs to relieve her anxiety.

These latchkey kids often call a parent at work to relieve their own anxieties or for the reassurance of hearing their parent's voice. Jay Belsky, a child development expert and professor at Pennsylvania State University, says, 'The issue is not so much if someone is there when a child gets home from school as much as whether someone is there psychologically for the child ... The psychological connection is more important than the physical one.'

Keeping in touch by phone can be overdone, however – and, of course, your employer may have a view on that too! If your

An estimated 800,000 children aged between five and 12 go home alone every day in the UK. The average parent receives four weeks' annual holiday; their children are out of school about 12 weeks of the year.

children are calling you at work frequently, it may be that you are relying too much on the phone in your relation-ship with your children. They may be trying to tell you that they need more of your personal attention. A phone call is no substitute for spending time with the people we love. However, using the telephone wisely is a key survival skill of strong, busy families.

Time: quality v quantity

In any discussion about spending time with our children, a debate will break out sooner or later over the relative merits of 'quality' or 'quantity'. Both the quality and the quantity of the time we spend with our children are important. It takes a certain quantity of time together for quality time to happen! But, if you don't have a lot of time to give your children on any particular day, here's some good counsel from the parenting advisors at the BBC: 'Never underestimate how much you can get out of just a few moment of concentrated time with your child. Even babies know and appreciate when they're being fully engaged with for their own sake. As they grow, nothing pleases children as much as a few moments of their parent's undivided attention.'

Sometimes just a few minutes with our children can be real quality time – if we're really focused on them. Some evenings when our boys were younger, I tried to remember to put down my work for ten to 15 minutes for a quick board game with them. I usually enjoyed the break and they usually enjoyed beating me! In the middle of one of those quality time games with my younger son, he suddenly stopped playing to launch into a seemingly endless, intricately detailed account of something that happened that day in school. 'Come on, now,' I said, 'Either play the game or quit.' Physically I was there, but my mind and heart wanted to get the game over so I could go back to my oh-so-important work. I was not emotionally available to my son; not really *there* to be with him and enjoy him.

> 'I think the world today is upside down and is suffering so much because there is so little love in the homes and in family life. We have no time for our children, we have no time for each other. There is no time to enjoy each other.'
> *Mother Teresa*

When our children ask for our time, they invite us to join them in their world. That tells us that they love us and they need us. What wonderful affirmation that is! And, by accepting their request, we return that same affirming love to them through the gift of our time and our undivided attention. Whenever possible, it should not be diluted by thoughts of the sales meeting tomorrow or the sports event on TV. If it is truly to be a gift to our children, it must be a gift of *all* of ourselves.

In the car

Your son has a football game, your daughter wants to visit a school friend and your youngest child needs picking up from the childminder. You feel like a chauffeur – and you are. It can seem like we waste a lot of time in the car; time we could be spending with our family.

But wait! Who is in the car with you? Probably at least one of your children.

If a child lives with criticism, he learns to condemn.
If a child lives with hostility, he learns to fight.
If a child lives with ridicule, he learns to be shy.
If a child lives with fear, he learns to be apprehensive.
If a child lives with shame, he learns to feel guilty.
If a child lives with tolerance, he learns to be patient.
If a child lives with encouragement he learns to be confident.
If a child lives with acceptance, he learns to love.
If a child lives with recognition, he learns it is good to have a goal.
If a child lives with honesty he learns what truth is.
If a child lives with fairness, he learns justice.
If a child lives with security, he learns to have faith in himself and those about him.
If a child lives with friendliness, he learns the world is a nice place in which to live to love and be loved.

Anonymous

What are you doing, beside driving somewhere? Are you listening to the radio? This 15 or 20 minute trip together could be time redeemed from just chauffeuring to become time *together*.

A car journey can be a small piece of quality time. You've got your child 'captive' for those few minutes. Get into the habit of turning the radio off and starting a conversation. Maybe there's something your child has been wanting to ask you but it's never been the right time. Or you can talk about anything of interest to your child: how their team is doing, what latest fashions everyone is wearing or what they like best about a new friend. It may take a few trips for your child to get the message that talking together really is what's going to happen, but don't give up. Be prepared with a few questions or comments to get the conversation going.

Strong families are just as busy as any others – but they've learned how to take time and make time to enjoy each other, stay connected and strengthen their relationships.

Building survival skills 1: Surviving the time crunch and staying connected

Perhaps your family is feeling the 'family time famine'. Use these questions to see how well your family is surviving the time crunch and how you could do even better!

1   Recalling that there is meant to be 'a time for ... every activity under heaven' (Ecclesiastes 3:1), what family activities – perhaps now neglected – should you have time for?

2   Identify two or three time-related pressures on your family. How could you apply the ideas in this chapter to relieve some of those pressures and stengthen your family?

3   What opportunities are there in your family schedule that you can use more effectively to strengthen your family?

4   If there are times when your children need you to be available to them but you can't physically be present, what strategies (such as using the telephone) can you develop to improve communication?

5   What are some ways you can use your weekend time more effectively for the benefit of your family?

6   How have you made it clear to your spouse and children that they are your number one priority? If you are not sure, outline some steps here.

2 Creating and enjoying the family Sabbath

MASTERING OUR time with our families will surely have a positive impact on our family life. Examining our priorities and cutting back activities and commitments outside our homes will certainly give us more time to be at home with the family. But there is another strategy that hurried, time-starved families can adopt to find real rest and refreshment without simply dropping out or taking a prolonged vacation. It involves simply stopping and resting for one whole day each week to observe a family Sabbath.

The command to take one day in every seven for rest, refreshment and worship is a gift from God to his people in the Ten Commandments (Exodus 20). For the ancients, day after day was filled with strenuous, unceasing work for all but a very few. The Sabbath was a command, but also a gift; an invitation to regularly stop work, rest and be refreshed in body and soul.

Even a person's servants and animals were entitled to rest on the seventh day, for God himself had completed the work of creation on that day and declared it holy. But, although the Sabbath was to be a day of resting, it was not to be a day of sheer idleness. It was also a day of 'sacred assembly', of worship, a day that offered God's people spiritual refreshment as well as physical rest (Leviticus 23:3). Both are a vital part of the gift of the Sabbath; it's impossible to rest our bodies well if our spirits are not also at peace.

The Sabbath offers the gift of rest to busy, exhausted

families today. And it's a gift they certainly need. So why do so few families take this gift?

'I justify my existence...'

When people ask me what I do for a living, I sometimes begin by saying (with a smile), 'I justify my existence by writing and editing'. For many – if not most – adults, work not only supports us but seems necessary to 'justify' our existence. We work not only to eat but to feel significant, needed. If we're busy, our lives are justified.

The harder we work, the more important and justified we feel. That's why it's so difficult to slow down and cut back. Every summer on holiday at the coast, I see (and hear!) men and women lying on their beach towels while talking business on their mobile phones. They can't detach themselves from their work for a week and just relax. Is it because of the need to feel important, indispensable, justified?

Our western industrialised culture trumpets this message daily: work is where the important things in life are accomplished. That's where the action is. The really important people are the ones who make work their first priority. And where do families fit in? Largely, they don't. They're supposed to take the leftovers of our time and energy. They really aren't that important. To paraphrase an old saying, 'If your employer wanted you to have a family, he'd have issued you one.'

> Remember the Sabbath day by keeping it holy. Six days you shall labour and do all your work, but the seventh day is a Sabbath to the LORD your God. On it you shall not do any work, neither you, nor your son or daughter...
> *Exodus 20:8–10*

If we're going to reclaim time for family life, we'll need to develop disciplines to help us slow down and keep our priorities in proper perspective. Observing a family Sabbath will help us do just that.

A holiday with God

In her very readable book, *Sabbath Keeping: Finding Freedom in the Rhythms of Rest*, Lynne Baab tells of speaking to a group of tired, stressed-out mothers of pre-school children. They told her of the 'seven-days-a-week pressure' they're under to keep countless activities going: driving kids around, keeping the home organised and clean, cooking, shopping for food, and trying to give their kids some significant time and attention too. When Baab told them about the rewards of stopping their frantic pace one day each week, one mother blurted out, 'I didn't know I was allowed to rest.'

The Sabbath offers us the gift of a weekly holiday with God. Setting aside one day in every seven to slow down and rest is a rhythm that's built into our very beings by our Creator.

Our Creator knows what we need and knows how reluctant we are to take it. So he *commands* that we take his gift of the Sabbath. It's a command – but it's also a gift. It's a gift to the tired, stressed-out mother who didn't know she was allowed to rest. It's a gift to the exhausted, frustrated father who just can't find the time or the energy to have fun with his young children. It's a gift to families who need permission to slow down.

> ... he said to them, 'The Sabbath was made for man, not man for the Sabbath.'
> *Mark 2:27*

Without that weekly pattern of work and rest, we become machines of production rather than joyful children of the God who created and redeemed us.

A threatening idea

Keeping a Sabbath can be an uncomfortable, even threatening, idea. In a way, a family Sabbath calls us voluntarily to give up control of our fate for one entire day and recognise that our future is in God's hands, not ours. But the Sabbath also gently reminds us that we don't have to justify our existence; we can't earn God's love by all our frantic exertion and, in fact, we don't need to.

The Sabbath is a day to turn from the things that occupy our working days and participate in activities that are about relationship, worship, celebration and thankfulness. Eugene Peterson calls the Sabbath that 'uncluttered time and space in which we can distance ourselves from our own activities enough to see what God is doing.'

He adds, 'If we are not able to rest one day a week, we are taking ourselves far too seriously.' And that's a trap many of us adults living fast-paced lives in high-pressured jobs surely fall into!

A conference at the Royal Society of Medicine in London in 2002 reported that the increasing 24/7 culture was posing a health risk. Long work hours and increasing leisure activities was disturbing sleep patterns, causing negative effects on mood and performance, difficulties regulating blood sugar levels, heart and stomach problems. Britons were sleeping on average six hours a night rather than the recommended eight.

The Sabbath offers us a weekly opportunity to step back from a secular culture that glorifies the workplace and threatens our families so that we can take time to refocus our priorities on the things that really matter. It helps us clear away the distractions of life so we can rest – truly rest – in God and be refreshed in both body and spirit.

'You must be kidding!'

'You must be kidding!' may well be your reaction. 'How can taking one whole day off each week help our family have more time and energy to enjoy each other? It doesn't make sense. Won't we just get further behind and be more stressed and frustrated as a result?'

That would seem to be the logical conclusion, wouldn't it? But remember, the Sabbath isn't just a command; it's a gift, given for our good. If we're too busy to take that gift, too busy to observe a weekly family Sabbath, we're too busy!

Yes, there may seem to be a risk involved. But all I can say is that many of the families who have incorporated a weekly Sabbath into their lives have found that they actually have *more* energy at work and can accomplish as much or more there *and* at home than if they didn't observe a weekly Sabbath. More than one family has discovered that, as they began to keep the Sabbath, 'we found ourselves with more time, not less. Don't ask how; it's one of those miraculous things!'

As we enter into the rest of one day in seven, we find that – in some good and mysterious way – God multiplies our time and energy so that we gain, rather than lose. God refills our physical, emotional and spiritual tanks on that one day so that we are free to give more to the other six. That's not the motivation for observing a Sabbath, of course. The benefits of a Sabbath are far greater than just an increase in efficiency or productivity. We honour the Sabbath to honour the God who commanded it. But, is it surprising that God honours those who honour him?

Not just for stressed-out adults

A family Sabbath is most certainly not just for adults. Many children lead over-scheduled, stressful lives, too. They need the gift of the Sabbath as much as their parents. They may not be aware of it but, as they hurry from activity to activity, children get the same message from our culture that adults do: the greatest human value and benefits are found in being busy and productive. Our children need permission to slow down, rest and take time to have a relationship with God, just as we do. The family Sabbath gives them that permission.

And parents who model rest, worship and celebration one day out of seven enable their children to accept the gift of the Sabbath joyfully and without guilt.

Questions! Questions!

If the idea of a weekly family Sabbath is new to you, you've probably got lots of questions:
- When should our family keep the Sabbath?
- What if Sunday is impossible for us?
- What can and can't we do on our Sabbath?
- How should we make it special and not just a boring day of enforced inactivity?

Remember: the Sabbath is a good gift from God, not just another obligation. It's not helpful to get bogged down in legalisms and focus all our energies on Sabbath dos and don'ts. Our rule is the one Jesus followed:' … The Sabbath was made for people, not people for the Sabbath' (Mark 2:27).

So, when is the right time to observe a family Sabbath? Most families will probably want to choose Sunday. Over the centuries, Christians have chosen to observe the Sabbath on the first day of the week in celebration of the Lord's resurrection that day. Even though Sunday has become largely indistinguishable from Saturday as just another weekend day of errands and shopping, it is still the time when most Christians gather for worship. So if you can observe your family Sabbath on Sunday, you can benefit from both physical rest and spiritual renewal on that same day. In fact, corporate worship has been part of Sabbath observance from the very beginning (Leviticus 23:3).

But some family members have to work at weekends or have shifts that include Sundays. Is that wrong? Can they still observe a family Sabbath? Just as Jesus recognised that 'the Sabbath was made for people', he also recognised that there were certain activities that couldn't responsibly be avoided on the Sabbath. Animals have to be cared for. People need to eat. Good deeds are always appropriate (Matthew 12:1–12).

I grew up on a dairy farm in New York state. My father believed strongly in honouring God by honouring the Sabbath, but he knew that cows needed to be milked twice daily. You couldn't decide not to milk them on Sunday. They would be very uncomfortable with udders full of milk and likely to develop infections; the cows would become sick and good milk lost. To let this happen would not be kind to his cows or good stewardship of them and their milk. So my father milked his cows on Sunday without guilt, but he didn't plough or harvest or do any work that was avoidable on Sunday.

When it's not possible to observe the Sabbath on Sunday, look for an alternative. For example, you can follow the Jewish practice of observing the Sabbath from sunset on Friday to sunset on Saturday. Or perhaps early Saturday afternoon until early Sunday afternoon will fit your schedule. Think about it carefully, talk it over together, pray about it; then experiment and see what works best.

If your family can't worship together on Sunday, again explore alternatives. The church where I worship holds a Thursday evening worship service called 'the first service of the weekend'. It features the same sermon and theme as the Sunday worship and it's aimed at people who have to work

> Weekend working is having an adverse effect on families across Britain, particularly on disadvantaged households. The National Centre for Social Research reveals that around 1.4 million parents are working regularly through the whole weekend and over 2.5 million families are affected by a parent working regularly over the weekend.
>
> Research by the Joseph Rowntree Foundation found that 75 per cent of workers who work weekends do not do so out of choice. Among mothers in this group, 78 per cent said that they were dissatisfied with working on Sundays.

on Sunday or will be away that weekend.

Getting started

If you and your family are really going to rest and be refreshed on your Sabbath, you'll need to do some careful planning and preparation. Make a list of the things you usually do during the time you've set aside. Which of those do not contribute to your rest, relaxation and focus on God? Which don't you really enjoy? Which don't promote a sense of the specialness of the day? Can you eliminate those from your Sabbath with some advance planning? Can you do your laundry, clean your house or run your errands earlier in the week so that the Sabbath is free of chores?

Then, make your family Sabbath a special time – a time of celebration! You may want to use some traditional Jewish Sabbath practices. For example, the Jewish Sabbath typically begins with lighting candles and saying a brief prayer to welcome the Sabbath. You might choose to read a psalm of praise and thanksgiving. You may want to have a special meal that features family members' favourite foods – perhaps served on the best china! Perhaps you'll want to celebrate by having friends over or playing a favourite game. Develop family rituals that help your family slow down and focus on God and each other.

The end of your Sabbath celebration can be special also. You could offer a prayer of thanks to God for the gift and joys of the Sabbath just ended. Don't forget to let your children read or improvise prayers and participate actively in the celebration rituals. As we'll see later, rituals have a strong appeal to children. Spiritual rituals are a powerful aid to both children and adults in focusing on God.

What shouldn't I do?

It's easy to fall into the trap of making a family Sabbath a joyless, legalistic obligation – and that would be sad indeed. That was the mistake some of the religious leaders of Jesus' time made. They were so concerned about what to do and not do on the Sabbath that they developed scores of burdensome rules that robbed the Sabbath of its restorative, life-giving power. Jesus told them they had it all wrong (Matthew 12:1–12).

Sadly, many families – even those who go to church on Sunday – make the Sabbath little different from the other six days of the week. After church they carry on with jobs around the house or shopping trips. It's hardly a restful or special day.

So how do you decide what to do or not do on the Sabbath? I like the criteria used by a rabbi. He asked three questions:

- Does it promote rest and relaxation?
- Does it bring delight and enjoyment?
- Does it give you a sense of holiness and sanctity?

Some activities only need to secure a 'yes' to one question, but the most fulfilling Sabbath activities earn a 'yes' to all three.

My wife finds gardening relaxing. She is renewed by just having her hands in the soil. It reminds her of the goodness of God's provision in creation. Time working in the garden is one good way for her to celebrate a Sabbath. I'm quite different. I very much dislike gardening and would much rather read a good book or go for a walk or a bike ride. Each of us needs to chooses activities which help us observe the spirit and purpose of the Sabbath. What does your family enjoy doing that you don't have time for during the rest of the week?

But what about playing sports on the Sabbath? If football practice or other sports commitments have taken over your Sundays, why not have your family Sabbath on Saturday? And while you're at it, why not start a petition to get the sports events moved. Reclaim Sunday for families! The situation gets even more complex if dad or mum have to work on a Saturday or Sunday.

What about shopping on your Sabbath? Again, I don't want to get legalistic. But, although some families enjoy shopping expeditions together, much of our shopping falls under the category of 'must do' and those things are generally not restful! In addition, there are benefits to staying out of the shops one day a week; that one day away from the shopping centres reminds us and our children that life is much more than what you can buy. It helps us pull back from the pressures of commercialism and acquisition. That time shopping could be spent walking, playing or eating together; in other words, enjoying time together as a family.

Little to lose, much to gain

Are you ready to slow down your life enough to observe a weekly family Sabbath? What have you got to lose besides exhaustion and stress? And there's so much for your family to gain. Do you want to spend more time with God, in prayer or in reading his Word? Observing the Sabbath is a weekly reminder that God is to be first in our lives and a weekly aid to making that a reality. Do you wish you had time for deeper friendships? The Sabbath offers the time and space needed to grow deep, lasting relationships with family, friends, neighbours. Do you wish your family was closer, more united, less just a collection of individuals living under the same roof? Keeping the Sabbath will promote family unity. We can establish family traditions that hold us together and build a store of good memories.

A family Sabbath wondrously, even miraculously, helps us overcome the 'family time famine' that fragments and weakens our families. Take it and enjoy it as a good gift from God.

Building survival skills 2: Creating and enjoying the family Sabbath

Observing a family Sabbath may require some serious discussions and careful planning. These questions are designed to help you get started!

1 Identify areas in which your family is over-scheduled and time-starved. What priorities do these situations reflect?

2 ' ... The Sabbath was made for man, not man for the Sabbath' (Mark 2:27). How do these words of Jesus change your attitude towards, or understanding of, the Sabbath in any way?

3 What benefits do you see for your family from observing a family Sabbath? What changes in your weekly routines would be required?

4 What obstacles stand in the way? How might you begin to tackle them?

5 What part will worship play in your family Sabbath?

6 How and when will you discuss and plan for a family Sabbath with the rest of the family? When could you begin to put your plans into action?

3 Balancing work and family

- IN JUNE 2003 rising political star Alan Milburn resigned his office of Health Secretary in the UK government to 'spend more time with his family'. He said he was finding it difficult to balance a frontbench Westminster career with the needs of his two young sons in the north east of England. Yet not many months passed before he was back in the political limelight.

- Prime Minister Tony Blair has been reported as liking to get home early in the evening to see his young son Leo.

- In the US in October 2004 the Head of Cybersecurity Amit Yoran resigned three months after the birth of his twins to become more involved in their upbringing.

- Karen Hughes, one of President Bush's closest advisors, suddenly resigned her powerful position in 2002 to move home to Texas, having found that the demands of her job kept her away too much from her children.

These headline stories reveal something of the frustration of the struggle with the work and family life balance. So let's look more closely at some of the negative effects of the long-hours culture on families.

Time crunch is universal

Over half of full-time workers in the UK would prefer to work fewer hours. And as many as eight out of ten working parents in the US say they would be willing to accept lower pay and slower advancement in exchange for working fewer hours and gaining a measure of control over their work schedule.

The 'time crunch' is universal. Parents in the US spend up to 40 per cent less time with their children today than they did 40 years ago. The same UK survey quoted in the panel goes on to suggest that parents 'are not content with the amount of time they are able to spend with their children, reading, playing and helping them with their homework'. One study found that over half of full-time workers were concerned about having too little time with their families, with a quarter believing it was impossible to have a good family life if they were to progress in their current job.

Most two-parent families in the UK are also two-earner families, and the government expects that trend to continue. More than half of single parents go out to work, with a government target for that to reach 70 per cent by 2010. In both Europe and the US, almost all the additional employment rate in the past decade has been provided by women entering the labour market – many of them mothers. A DTI (Department of Trade & Industry) report says: 'Helping mothers and fathers to balance work and family life can … have positive impacts on children's health, schooling and prospects in later life… Difficulties in managing this [work-life] balance can have a detrimental impact on the quality of relationships between parents and children and the parent's responsiveness to the child, with implications for child outcomes.'

The idolatry of work

Arlie Hochschild and Annie Machung, authors of *The Second Shift*, a book about two-career families, point out: '… for all the talk about the importance of children, the cultural climate has become subtly less hospitable to parents who put children first. This is not because parents love children less, but because a *job culture* has expanded at the expense of a *family culture*.'

The 'job culture' defines *work* as the activity which gives life its greatest meaning and most significant rewards. As a result, work takes precedence over all other demands on our time, including family. This is nothing less than the *idolatry of work* and should be seen for what it really is: a dangerous attack on the family.

Surviving in such a family-hostile culture will require families of faith to refuse to bow to the idol of work, to be constantly vigilant against sacrificing the joys of family life on its altar and, with the support of other families and their communities of faith, to pioneer a truly balanced lifestyle that honours both family and work as gifts from God. That's a big challenge, but there are choices available today that can help families meet it.

Since October 1998 the *Working Time Directive* has been law in the UK. With a few exclusions, this sets a maximum working week of 48 hours averaged over a rolling 17-week period, weekly rest periods of 24 hours and daily rest periods of 11 hours, and a guaranteed three weeks' holiday. However, research by the Insititute for Employment Studies reveals that British employees work some of the longest hours in Europe, regularly working more than ten hours a week over and above their contracted hours.

Flexible working arrangements

Parents today are demanding a greater measure of control over their work schedules so that they can better balance work and family responsibilities. And, in fact, they are able to choose from a whole range of options that will enable them to do just that.

Flexitime (or flextime) is growing in popularity throughout the western world. In the UK about two and a half million employees work flexible hours. Flexitime usually assumes a stand-ard number of hours to be worked each day but allows employees to vary their actual working hours

2006 figures revealed that 48 per cent of UK employers offer flexitime – a considerably lower percentage than other countries; for example Germany (90 per cent) and Sweden (94 per cent). Part-time working is offered by 97 per cent of UK employers, jobsharing is offered by 55 per cent, homeworking by 32 per cent and teleworking by 20 per cent.

around a core time when presence in the workplace is required. So, in an office with a core time of 10am to 3pm, if you had to drop off children for daycare at 8am, you could work from 9am to 5pm that day. You might arrange to work 7am to 3pm because you needed to take your child to a late afternoon clinic visit or attend another child's sports event.

Many major firms are now offering flexible working. All HSBC employees, for example, have the right to request flexible working arrangements (not just those with children under six years, as required by law). The company says no employee should feel guilty for requesting flexible working; a recent survey showed that 75 per cent of HSBC employees agreed that their workload allows them to keep their work and family life in good balance. HSBC also has an extensive nursery network providing parents with up to 50 per cent off the usual nursery costs.

A report in *The Scotsman* in June 2006 said that flexitime was not just being sought by women with young children: 'People from Generation Y – those among the workforce born after 1978 – are unafraid to demand not only good corporate responsibility from their employers, but flexible hours too. And ... a happier ... workforce costs less and produces more. Absenteeism costs British business at least £11.6 billion a year ... A recent study revealed that 70 per cent of senior executives who were in a job-share were generating 30 per cent more output than one person doing the same time ... 85 per cent of human resources managers believe allowing flexitime improves both morale and motivation among staff ... British Telecom ... now have people working from home and found these employees were 31 per cent more productive than their office-bound colleagues.'

Mark, a programme manager for MSN-UK, works 7:30am to 3:30pm so he can spend time with his new baby and give his wife a break when he gets home. His manager has assured him that flexible working will have no negative impact on his prospects with the company.

Flexitime still requires a full day's work, so it may not free up any more actual time for working parents to spend with their children. But it may allow parents to spend more 'prime time' daylight hours with their children without the financial sacrifices that part-time work entails. Dr Kyle Pruett, Clinical Professor of Psychiatry at the Yale University Child Study Center, writes in *The Nurturing Father: Journey Towards the Complete Man* that flexitime 'may, in fact, be the most valuable of all the business solutions for the children because it permits parents to plan their time for childcare in ways *they* choose, not at the convenience of their employees. Such flexibility may, for example, eliminate the need for full-time daycare in some two-career families.' Interestingly, Pruett adds that flexitime 'is rated by many fathers as the most desirable work-related aid to their fathering.'

Other types of flexible working

Another flexible work arrangement is the *compressed work week*. An employee might work four days of ten hours and have three days off each week. A variation is the 9/80 schedule where the employee works 80 hours over nine days instead of the usual ten, earning an extra day off every second week. This allows parents the kind of flexibility and control over their work schedule that many want and need.

Job sharing is also an attractive option to some, especially women who want to work outside the home but want to have blocks of time available to their children. A common arrangement is for two people to cover one job with both working three days each week; two days separately and one day together to aid communciation and coordination.

Sarah went back to work from 8am to noon daily when her daughter was two and a half. Soon, it became clear that her job required full-time hours yet she still wanted to have time with her young daughter. Because her employer permits various kinds of flexible working arrangements, Sarah found another working mother, Emma, who also wanted to cut back to a part-time schedule. Now the two women share one full-time job. Sarah works Monday to Wednesday and Emma works Wednesday to Friday.

Despite its benefits, formal job sharing still involves only a tiny part of the workforce. And, for many single parents, job sharing – essentially a part-time option – may not be viable for financial reasons.

There are other less familiar but promising flexible working options: *term-time working* (working full- or part-time only during the school calendar and taking unpaid leave during school holidays) and *working during school hours* only (an option still rarely offered in the US).

In the US, there is no legal right to flexitime but it is being offered by literally hundreds of large companies around the country. James, a manager of software development for IBM, has a flexitime arrangement that allows him to arrive at work after dropping the children off at daycare three days a week. On the other two days, he arrives earlier so he can leave the office promptly at 5pm. That way, James can pick up his children from day care, feed them and spend time with them before bedtime.

Today, 26 per cent of employees in the UK work part-time. The number, 7 million, has more than tripled in the past 35 years. Surveys show that most are women, and most work part-time because they choose to, not because they are forced to.

Part-time working is appealing but it is not without problems. Many, if not most, part-time jobs are in relatively low paid sectors, such as cleaning, retail, and food service. Since most part-time workers are women, part-time work can perpetuate stereotypical gender roles and consolidate the inferiority of women in the workplace in terms of pay and career opportunities. In the US this is called being put on the

'Mommy Track' – a decidedly second class career path. And part-time work is hardly an option for single parents who are the sole or main source of income for the family.

Working at home or telecommuting often appeals to parents wanting more time with their families. It also eliminates or reduces time-consuming and expensive travel. Most do freelance work such as providing family daycare, word processing or bookkeeping. Others run home-based businesses. 'Telecommuters' or 'teleworkers' are employed by a business but work at least part of the time at home. Some companies find it economical to hire people to answer customer calls at home (often during hours the employee can choose) rather than set up expensive call centres.

I'm a telecommuter, working at home, keeping in touch with my office by email and telephone. The advantages are obvious. My wife works full-time as a teacher but I was always home mid afternoon when our children came in from school and available in the hour or so until my wife arrived home. And teleworking also often offers the advantages of flexitime: the ability to adjust your hours some days to meet specific family needs.

The legal right to request flexible working arrangements is relatively new in the UK, having been introduced in 2003. This option presently applies only to parents caring for children under six (or under 18 if the child is disabled). But employers are required by law to consider any request seriously and reply within 14 days. There is even an appeal process when requests are denied. Similar legal rights to flexible working arrangements would be a great gift to working parents in the US too!

Parental leave

There's little debate over whether parental leave to care for newborns is a good thing. Most experts agree that parents and babies need time to bond. The growing availability and use of maternity and paternity leave is permitting that.

Throughout the UK all women employees have a legal right to 26 weeks of job-guaranteed maternity leave for birth or adoption, regardless of the hours worked or length of service (so it includes part-time workers) and they may be able to take as much as 52 weeks. All contractual rights such as pensions and holidays are protected during the leave.

Though this mandatory leave is unpaid, many women qualify for weekly Statutory Maternity Pay (providing for six weeks pay at 90 per cent of their average weekly salary) or a maternity allowance from the government. Paternity leave is not quite so liberal, but fathers are legally entitled to up to two weeks leave after the birth or adoption of a child and may be eligible for up to 56 days of leave and Statutory Paternity Pay also.

Some firms, however, are now offering parental leave beyond the legal requirements. Jaguar & Land Rover offers 52 weeks of maternity leave with full pay and the option of taking another year of unpaid leave – job guaranteed. The Penguin Group offers four weeks of paid paternity leave to new fathers as well as up to 15 days of compassionate leave for parents when their children or their children's carers are ill.

One NHS Trust offers both fathers and mothers two full weeks of paid parental leave after five years of employment. Phil, an administrative superintendant with this trust, took two weeks of paid paternity leave and two weeks' annual leave on the birth of his daughter so that he 'would not miss one bit of this important month' and 'felt able to play a key part in Rose's first month of development'.

Chris is a father who works for a bio-technology company. At 34, he took three months off work after his wife returned to work so he could get to know his infant son. It wasn't easy but he felt it was well worth it.

Again, the situation in the US is less favourable. Firms of 50 or more employees are required to offer 12 weeks of (unpaid) parental leave to all employees who have worked for the firm for at least one year and averaged at least 25 hours per week. The Family and Medical Leave Act of 1993 provides for fathers or mothers needing leave to care for a newborn of an adopted child or a seriously ill immediate family member, or to care for a personal, serious medical condition. But, again, the leave is unpaid.

'Help! I need child care'

The increase in employment of women and the growth of families where the woman is the sole provider has brought a growing demand for safe, affordable childcare.

Many parents rely on an informal network of family and friends to provide care. Others must turn to childminders, many of whom work from their home and are parents themselves. Some rely on day care centres such as nurseries (for pre-school children) or after-school clubs that offer care in the school building before and after school hours.

If you use someone outside of your informal network, you'll want to be sure to choose staff and environments meeting national standards. Individuals working with children need to have been checked and approved by the CRB (Criminal Records Bureau) in the UK. Choosing care from registered centres may also mean eligibility for tax credits to offset the costs if you work at least 16 hours a week. Single parents may also qualify for tax-free vouchers to pay childcare costs when they are looking for work or starting training.

Some larger employers offer on-site childcare. Others offer salary plans to help you pay childcare costs with tax-free funds. Finding the right childcare is still not easy, but help and options for working parents in the UK are increasing. The situation in the US is not so easy. The largest group of parents (35 per cent) use an informal network of family and friends or neighbours providing care in their homes, as my wife did when our children were young. About one in five pay a formal, organised day care facility. There are some government funds to help provide daycare for low income families and those trying to move off benefits. And there is a childcare tax credit available to low and middle income families. But actual cash help for many families is non-existent.

Some major US employers are trying to fill the gap. For example, at the Johnson & Johnson headquarters in New Brunswick, New Jersey, there is a sleek, white building with state-of-the-art equipment, including a computer lab. This building serves 200 clients, but they are not the company's usual customers. These clients range from six weeks to six years old. This is the corporate headquarters daycare centre.

For families with faith

Families with faith are not exempt from the many heavy job responsibilities that threaten to overwhelm family life and deprive us of its blessings. We struggle to maintain the right balance – and even to know what the right balance is. Like everyone else, we are prone to finding ourselves dominated by the long hours culture and the 'idolatry of work'.

Teach us to number our days aright, that we may gain a heart of wisdom.
Psalm 90:12

Here are two vital steps to help your family establish and maintain a healthy work/life balance:
- make careful, prayerful choices about when and how long to work;
- be willing to sacrifice income and promotion when they would weaken, not strengthen, your family.

Our faith gives us the foundation on which to make and maintain such choices. The example we set to other families is not insignificant. We can be pioneers who lead the way through this still largely uncharted territory of balancing work and family.

When a 'family-friendly' option such as flexible working or parental (especially paternity) leave is available and beneficial, let's take it. If the best employees – and Christian workers should be the best – demand the means to balance work and family, employers will be motivated to grant them. We need to assert the priority of people over production, the inestimable value of children, and the worthiness of self-sacrifice for the good of family. If we do, the benefits will flow to all families and the entire society. This is a blessing families of faith can give to all families! Who better to lead the way than followers of Jesus Christ, the one who called children to his side and gave his life as a sacrifice for a world of people he deeply loves?

Building survival skills 3: Balancing work and family

For most families, the key to mastering time is maintaining a healthy balance between the demands of our jobs and the needs of our families. If your family is feeling out of balance right now, the questions below can help.

1   In what specific ways do you or your spouse experience the 'idolatry of work' and the conflict between the job culture and the needs of your family?

2   What options or choices does your employer (or your spouse's employer) offer that might help you achieve and maintain a greater balance? What sacrifices would be required? What benefits would be gained? What other options could you choose to take?

3   If your employer is not sympathetic to your needs to achieve a better work/home life balance, how might you persuade him about the benefits of more family-friendly working conditions?

4   How does your faith affect the way you approach your work/family struggles? Has reading this chapter given you ideas for some different strategies that might work for you? If it has, outline a timetable for putting at least one of those into operation.

5   If your goal is the wisdom that comes from 'numbering our days aright' (Psalm 90:12), how might holding to this ambition affect your work schedule and your participation in the long hours culture?

SURVIVAL SKILL 2

Building a strong family foundation

4 Growing a happy marriage

IT'S NOT AN original thought, but I agree heartily with the observation that nothing in life gives people as much happiness as a good marriage and as much misery as a bad one.

Everyone who is married, or ever hopes to be, wants a marriage that not only survives the many challenges it faces, but one that also produces happiness for both partners. That's actually one reason behind the high divorce rate today. People won't settle for *just* being married. They have high expectations; they want to be happy and they're determined to keep trying until they get it right!

That's really no surprise, is it? A happy marriage is a wellspring of three powerful gifts: sustenance, healing and growth. From a happy marriage we receive daily the sustenance and support of someone who truly cares for us. Our spouse's affection and acceptance helps heal the wounds we bear from childhood. These gifts enable us to believe that we are loved and valued, someone who matters, who belongs. The gift of personal growth is built on the security of a loving companion who is always there to encourage us to develop our gifts and talents, with all the satisfaction that brings us.

In both the US and UK between 40 and 50 per cent of marriages end in divorce, with the average length of time of those marriages at about 11 years. In the UK the most frequent reason why women are granted divorce is for 'unreasonable behaviour' by their husbands; for men divorcing the most common grounds is a separation of two years by their wives.

These are very precious gifts we can give our spouses daily

and are the stuff of which lasting, satisfying love is made. Marriage counsellors describe this kind of love as an 'intimate partnership' or a 'companionship love'. In practical terms, it's the kind of love shared by one couple interviewed after 40 years together. 'We're more than married,' they said. 'We're best friends.' This couple, and so many others like them, happily affirm that the central satisfaction of their lives is their marriage relationship!

Will the rubbish win?

Couples who are happily married invariably report that they grow their marriages in a number of crucial ways. One is by spending time together regularly. And they do it over the long haul. A happy marriage, of course, begins with the intention for just such a lifetime commitment. From a biblical perspective, marriage is the *basis* for love between a man and a woman, not the other way around. Ideally, love and marriage *should* go together, but – biblically – the marriage commitment takes priority, even over love. Tim Stafford, writing in an article in *Christianity Today,* puts it this way: 'The cup is necessary before the wine is poured.'

Unlike the microwave ready meal, an instant intimate partnership or companionship marriage is as impossible as an instant adult. The rewards of marriage are not instant. But patiently and deliberately dedicating yourself to the wellbeing of the one you love will, in time, bring a wonderful richness of relationship.

Nick Stinnett, in his book *Secrets of Strong Families,* tells the story of a couple who attended a marriage enrichment seminar. The leader asked them two questions: how many minutes they spent each week taking out the rubbish and how many minutes they spent each day in conversation. You've already guessed the result, I'm sure. The rubbish took about five minutes each day – and the rubbish won!

How can we be sure the rubbish doesn't win in the daily struggle to find time to grow happy marriages? There is no *easy* answer, but there is a way. It lies in the daily practice of some important marriage disciplines.

The daily disciplines of marriage

Suppose that we went on a trip around the country and stopped frequently along the way to talk with couples who have strong, happy marriages. What do you think we'd learn?

My guess is that we'd discover that these lasting, rewarding marriages all share at least one common characteristic: discipline. That's not a popular word in today's culture. But married couples can intentionally build into their lives many little habits and practices – many disciplines – that, in spite of the pressures of time and circumstances, enable their marriages to grow and deepen over the years.

Their lives are as busy as yours and mine. They don't have big blocks of time to just sit and gaze into each others' eyes. But they have discovered the value of some small things, done regularly, which make a big diference in their marriages. These daily disciplines of marriage have become a normal part of everyday life for them.

There are at least four such disciplines that are essential to building a lasting, rewarding marriage:
- keeping in touch;
- daily grace;
- growing together;
- growing in faith.

The discipline of keeping in touch

My wife and I have said many times over the years, 'It seems like I hardly knew you when we first got married.' After 35 years together, we realise how true that was!

The day we took our marriage vows, two strangers stepped

into a whole new world together. Like so many before and since, we started on a journey we hoped would last a lifetime and bring us great joy and satisfaction.

For most of us, marriage starts not only with these high hopes but with more than a dash of romance! Those early days together are sweetened by the romantic glow and excitement of beginning something tremendous together. Sooner or later, however, reality sets in – often linked to the arrival of children. Parenthood changes everything. Suddenly, we are responsible for a helpless little person. We are no longer on the receiving end of nurture from our spouse but become nurturers ourselves – quite a shock!

And, often, just at the time we have children, we're at the stage in life when our careers are getting more demanding. Something has to give. And sometimes that something is time and energy to keep the marriage alive and healthy.

As the demands of family life and careers increase from year to year, we may one day realise that we're no longer spending time on the little things of daily married life, such as conversation with our spouse, or just being available to listen in a caring way.

> *If love is the heartbeat of a marriage, communication is its lifeblood.*
> Opening sentence of a report on marriage enrichment by North Carolina State University

- 'We never talk anymore.'
- 'Okay… what do you want to talk about?'
- 'I don't know. I just want to talk.'

Does that sound familiar? We've had that conversation in our home. Perhaps you have, too. Even if you set aside time to talk, it may seem that there's nothing to talk about! That stranger you married some years ago and set out determined to have as your best friend is still (or once again) a stranger. If that happens, you've lost touch with each other. Your marriage is in jeopardy.

Talking and listening

Couples who want to cherish their marriage do so by practising the daily discipline of intentionally keeping in touch through sharing conversation (talking *and* listening) with each other. Sharing conversation includes more than the perfunctory 'How was your day?' that covers the 'battle report' on daily life. Marriage partners find they develop a 'soul intimacy' as they share, however briefly, their fears, hopes, doubts, desires and experiences of God's daily care. Of course, they don't neglect the progress reports on dental braces, sports games and that big sales presentation! They're important too. Without this shared conversation, involving little things as well as hopes and dreams, spouses can't be best friends, partners and companions.

It takes effort to do this regularly; effort to keep involved and interested enough in each other. It takes a real desire to keep each other filled in on the changes in our lives. That's why we call it a discipline.

Does this talk of daily disciplines sound too challenging? It needn't be. As little as five minutes of conversation to check in after work is a good beginning. A cup of coffee together after dinner (before washing up, the evening paper or the TV) or getting into bed a few minutes early to allow for some 'pillow talk' are simple examples of daily ways we can practise the discipline of keeping in touch with each other.

But this discipline goes well beyond just talking together, or even knowing what to say. It means knowing how to *listen*. It requires listening to the heart of our spouse so that we can discover together a common heart. This is the loving listening of two people on a journey toward a deep friendship and love.

Successful couples stay in touch with what made them fall for each other in the first place. They take time and make time to enjoy each other, to relive, recount and, periodically, re-kindle the romance between them.

And keeping in touch has a more literal aspect too. Jesus often put his hands on people as a means of blessing them and showing his love and care. Touch is a powerful communicator of those emotions. Physical intimacy – that quick hello hug or touch of the hand – helps keep romance alive and growing. Practise keeping in touch with your spouse this way, every day.

The discipline of daily grace

In his book *On This Day*, Carl D Windsor tells the story of a grandmother celebrating her golden wedding anniversary. Inevitably, someone asked her the secret of her long and happy marriage. She explained, 'On my wedding day, I decided to make a list of ten of my husband's faults, which, for the sake of our marriage, I would overlook.' When asked what some of those faults were, she replied, 'To tell you the truth, my dear, I never did get around to listing them. But whenever my husband did something that got me hopping mad, I would say to myself: Lucky for him that's one of the ten!'

> Love is patient, love is kind. It does not envy, it does not boast, it is not proud. It is not rude, it is not self-seeking; it is not easily angered, it keeps no record of wrongs.
>
> *1 Corinthians 13:4,5*

Here was a lady who was wise in the ways of marriage. She knew the need for grace in marriage to keep it happy and growing. In a study on marriage, psychologist Judith Wallerstein asked one woman, 'What makes for a successful marriage?' 'A bad memory,' was the reply. Wallerstein observed that being able to 'forget the day-to-day disappointments and focus on the bigger issues is what makes a marriage work.' Practising daily grace maintains a generally positive, rewarding atmosphere in marriage.

Occasions for grace

'Great occasions for serving God come seldom, but little ones surround us daily.' That's a saying I keep on my desk as a reminder of the need to show God's grace to my wife daily. Infrequently, if ever, will I be able to play the hero for my wife, but there are many small, yet significant, opportunities to serve God and show her his grace (and my love) every day.

It only takes a particularly stressful day (or week) at work or caring for a houseful of young children for two consecutive rainy days, for example, to remind us again how much the loving ministry of one spouse to another, the 'pitching in' and the thoughtful gesture, mean to our marriage.

Most mornings, my wife has to rush to get out of the house and into her car for the drive to work, while I 'commute' down the hall to my study. So, if she is behind schedule, hurrying to get dressed, I try to have her bowl of hot cereal waiting. In winter, I make sure that her car is snow free and the engine warmed before her commute begins.

My wife has *many* ways of ministering grace to me. For example, she knows I don't enjoy DIY, so there are many little jobs around the house that she fixes without even asking me to help. Now that's true grace!

Having a meal ready to serve when he gets home after a tiring conference... Filling the car with petrol because you know she's off to see her parents... Such things come as wonderful and undeserved reminders of our spouse's love. It's natural to focus on our own needs and the incessant demands of life that drain our energies minute by minute. The discipline of daily grace, by contrast, requires of us a deliberate dedication to the happiness and well-being of our spouse every day. That is the essence of Christian love which is essential to a happy, Christian marriage.

But this discipline of daily grace involves more than just

service. It involves accepting and forgiving our spouse daily too.

Acceptance and forgiveness

My wife keeps a neat, tidy house. The atmosphere is relaxed, the furniture functional. The house can be lived in and enjoyed, even by children. Yet, somehow, it remains clean and neat.

For me, however, a family home should have a newspaper or two and a few magazines casually spread around on any place big enough to hold them. I call that being 'lived in'. My wife calls it 'cluttered'. I have even been told that my desk looks like someone dumped their rubbish on it. But it feels very comfortable to me.

So you can see the potential for some sharp disagreements here! As a result, every day for our 35 years of marriage, my wife has had many opportunities to show me grace by accepting – as much as possible – my penchant for a 'lived in' home. And I have had the opportunity to show her grace by trying to be a bit neater! That's the way it is for most of us: daily acts of love and acceptance. It's grace. And it's a reflection of God's grace to us. After all, God does not wait until we are perfect to love and accept us. Loving our spouse means having a similar gracious willingness to love and accept them for who they are, without demanding that they first be perfect.

Grace and perspective

Farmers and diamond miners both move a lot of dirt in the course of a day, but their perspective is quite different. The farmer's main focus is on the dirt as he prepares it for the crops. The diamond miner's attention is focused not on the dirt but on the occasional diamond he finds there. He sees his work from the perspective of one concerned for the diamonds, not the dirt.

That's a helpful way to think about marriage and family life. What we look for in our spouse (or children) often determines what we find. There is inevitably a lot of 'dirt' to be sorted through in marriage; a lot of bad habits, disagreements and the like. Practising the discipline of daily grace towards our spouse doesn't necessarily mean we ignore the dirt. It just helps us keep it in perspective. We focus on the diamonds in our marriage: a caring husband or wife, a growing relationship, and daily acts of love and sharing that enrich our lives.

One of the first shocks many newly married people experience is realising that their spouse is far from perfect. It's hard for couples to see each other's weakness and flaws when blinded by new love. Each sees the other as perfect in every way! It isn't long, however, before reality sets in.

In this life, perfection is impossible, so, as Ruth Graham, wife of evangelist Billy Graham, observed, 'A good marriage is the union of two forgivers'. Daily applications of acceptance and forgiveness heal hurts and relieve resentments. They restore a spouse's bruised spirit, help keep it healthy and promote growth.

The discipline of growing together

For weeks it was the subject of screaming tabloid headlines and features on the evening news. Billionaire Donald Trump and his wife were getting a divorce. Here was a couple that seemed to have everything. What was the problem?

'People just grow apart,' Trump said. Both he and his wife were very busy people in stressful careers. He spent his married life amassing his fortune. She spent it managing one of his major hotels. Both of them were usually too busy or too stressed (or both) to spend time and energy being together. So they just grew apart.

Trump was right. Marriage partners *do* grow apart unless

they intentionally work at growing together. Few of us are as wealthy as the Trumps but our lives are not that different in at least one way: pressures from our careers and other commitments make it a real challenge for us to find time to enjoy being with each other regularly.

Yet, after a shared commitment to Christ, regular time together with our spouse is perhaps the most basic ingredient in growing together in marriage. How else are we going to get to know and be best friends with that stranger we married? Here are a couple of ideas to help you make that happen.

- Meal times: Making time to be together regularly may be as simple as spending a few minutes together over coffee after supper (after the children have left the table) or deliberately doing the washing-up together. Automatic dishwashers save time but may not be so good for marriages. That endangered species known as family mealtime isn't just good for the children. It provides a built-in daily time for marriage partners to keep in touch with each other too.
- Phone, text, email: A brief call or quick email to your spouse during a break at work is a great way to keep a feeling of closeness during the day. When my wife was on leave from her teaching career to care for our pre-school sons at home, we both looked forward to my daily call home while I was on my lunch break.
- Housework: I admit that I'm like most husbands in two-salary families – often guilty of not doing my share of the housework. But I have found there is something wonderfully therapeutic for me about vacuuming. And it matches my household skill level perfectly! So, during the weekly Saturday morning cleaning at our home, I vacuum while my wife does other cleaning chores. Cleaning is sometimes shared time – and we enjoy it.

Ice cream cone or sundae?

The story is told of a couple whose house was hit by a tornado. The roof lifted off and the bed on which the couple was sleeping was swept up and gently set down a few miles away. The wife began to cry. Her husband, trying to comfort her, said, 'Don't cry, honey. We're OK.'

'I'm not crying because I'm scared,' the wife said. 'I'm crying with happiness. This is the first time in 15 years we've been out together.'

When I was a child, going out for ice cream was one of our family's favourite activities. We could all choose a delicious scoop of our favourite flavour. I remember, however, that it wasn't too long before I began to wish for more than just one scoop in a cone. I wanted a big, delicious sundae!

Our small daily times together with each other are like those delicious single scoop cones. They're always special, but they also whet our appetite for those longer 'just the two of us' times together.

Bob and Cheryl have been married for over a quarter of a century. They still hold hands a lot, laugh together and clearly enjoy simply being with one another. Why haven't things become stale? What's their secret? Throughout their marriage, they've kept Friday evening for each other. It's their time to just be together and sometimes to go out on a date. Bob and Cheryl value that regular, weekly date highly because they have learned from experience that time together alone – without the kids – can keep the flame of marital love burning.

Did you notice the part about 'without the kids'? That can be the hardest part of arranging dates. Every parent knows that finding the time, the money and the energy to focus on each other can seem impossible when there are young children involved.

My advice is: do whatever it takes to make those dates happen! Plan ahead. Write the date in your calendar so that work and other obligations can't easily interfere. Budget for a babysitter once a week or twice a month. Try to get away together a couple of times each year for a night or two.

Some couples enjoy spending time together on joint projects, whether that's working on a garden makeover, serving together at a city mission, going to an evening class or restoring old furniture. We live in New York state, not far from the border with Massachusetts and Vermont, and we enjoy every opportunity we have to drive over and explore the many beautiful New England towns close by.

> The one thing children wear out faster than shoes is parents.
> *John J Plomp*

Your date with your spouse is limited only by your own creativity. Take a candlelight bath together late one evening. Sit outside in the moonlight together. Take a bike ride. Visit a local museum. Do the supermarket run together. Go for a walk in the snow, followed by a hot shower together. Plan a quiet dinner: sit with the children while they eat, put them to bed and then break out the candles!

Donald Trump was only partly right. People don't need to 'just grow apart'. They can *grow together* into an ever-deepening love and companionship. You can, too. Start small, if necessary – but start now. Small investments made regularly will grow and yield a large reward: a strong, happy marriage.

The discipline of growing in faith

I believe it is a spiritual principle: as you deepen your discipleship you strengthen your marriage. Nothing creates such a strong and lasting marriage bond as a deeply held and shared allegiance to Jesus Christ.

And a shared faith is a key element in helping couples keep their wedding vows of lifelong fidelity – which is, after all, God's plan and purpose for marriage. In marriage, spouses are to enjoy the blessings of an exclusive relationship 'never to be shared with strangers' (Proverbs 5:17). Jesus' own words make it clear: marriage is God's gift to a man and a woman who become 'one flesh' and are not to be separated by anyone or anything except death (Matthew 19:4–6).

How can couples nurture a strong, shared faith that assures fidelity and endures for a lifetime? Some couples may start the day just ten or 15 minutes earlier (before the children) so that they can have a cup of coffee and sing a hymn or praise song together as a couple. Other couples may pray and have a brief daily quiet time with God; some together, some individually.

Couples who are growing in faith together make it a priority to worship together, especially in their local church community. They live out their faith together through the rituals and traditions of the many seasons of the Church year. In this way, they develop a shared faith history and identity as a couple.

These couples don't just 'talk' their faith, they 'walk' it too. They serve their Lord together at the community soup kitchen or homeless shelter, or set an example of pastoral care as they lead their neighbourhood small group.

Couples in strong Christian families undertake willingly the task of sharing their faith with their growing children too. And they do it in the most effective way ever discovered: by being models and teachers of their children through their daily life together as a family. We'll talk about that in more detail in another chapter. Right now it's enough to recognise that this task alone is enough to keep any couple on their toes and growing together spiritually.

If you're someone who feels you've not put enough effort

into growing together in faith with your spouse, don't despair. It's never too late. Here, too, you can start small. The important thing is to start. God will honour your faithful efforts. If you're starting from scratch, perhaps you'll want to begin by having your own, personal daily time with God for reading the Bible and prayer. If your spouse doesn't share that daily discipline, be patient, and share with him or her occasionally how much it means to your daily growth in faith.

A thorny issue: who's in charge?

Any couple hoping to have a lasting, rewarding marriage has to resolve at least one contentious issue: when decisions have to be made, who's in charge? When we disagree, who makes the final decision? Because, after all, someone has to! For many years, the answer to these questions has usually been 'the husband'. The husband, it was argued, was the God-appointed head of the family because he is the 'head of the wife as Christ is head of the Church' (1 Corinthians 11:3; Ephesians 5:23). But what a heavy burden that puts on husbands! They always have to be right; to know everything.

Submit to one another out of reverence for Christ.
Ephesians 5:21

What about when the wife has more expertise or insight? Should wives have to deny or suppress what they know is right, perhaps at great self sacrifice, in order to obey the command to 'submit to … [their] husbands as to the Lord' (Ephesians 5:22)?

In recent years, however, sincere Christians have come to disagree on whether the Bible requires this patriarchal marriage relationship with the husband as the boss (however loving). Some, like me, believe the Bible offers a very different model for the marriage relationship; one you might call 'mutual submission' or 'equal partnership'.

What does it mean that the husband is 'head of the wife as Christ is head of the Church'? At the time the New Testament was written, the word for 'head' was not primarily used to refer to a boss or authority. It most often referred to a 'source' – as in the 'head' of a river. It meant the starting point for life or the source that produces or grows life. Christ, as head of the Church, functions this way and provides the Church with both guidance and power.

From this perspective, the husband as head has a wonderful, Christ-like function in the marriage: to empower his wife's growth in Christ to become all God wants her to be. Men and women are 'joint heirs' of God's grace (1 Peter 3:7).

In general, Christians are called to be slaves of each other (Galatians 5:13) and consider the interests of others above their own (Philippians 2:3,4). Is this compatible with a marriage where one spouse is the boss and the other simply submits?

I believe that the overall teaching of the Bible permits us, if not requires us, to reject the hierarchical model for marriage. From both my study of the Bible and 35 years of marriage I believe that an equal partnership model, characterised by mutual submission of each partner to the other, promotes a healthier marriage more in line with what the Bible teaches.

Not incidentally, 'equal partnership marriage' is more likely to lead to 'equal partnership parenting'. Equal parenting usually means more involvement from dad, which is a great benefit for the children. After all, the Bible never says mothering is more valuable than fathering!

So when couples disagree, who makes the decision? Doesn't someone have to 'make the call'? Yes and no! Yes, a decision has to be made – but no, it doesn't have to be the same person each time. Spouses may agree that, in certain instances, one or the other spouse will make the decision, perhaps based on expertise or stronger feelings. So, some*one* doesn't have to make the decision. In the face of disagreement, a couple may choose to do the hard work of listening to each other, praying, respecting each other's opinions and taking the time to let God lead them to a joint decision. They 'mutually submit' to each other. It's hard work. It's another marriage discipline. But in the end it leads to a stronger, more rewarding marriage.

Living in a mismatched marriage

There are many marriages where, for any number of reasons, one spouse has a living Christian faith and the other spouse's faith is non-existent. Some marry as non-believers and one comes to faith some time later. Some marry knowing their spouse doesn't share their faith but certain they'll 'win them over'. Some may be deceived by a partner who only pretends to have faith. For either spouse this can be, as one woman described it, 'like living with an alien'. For the believing spouse, such a marriage can be the source of much pain, grief, guilt, frustration, anger and even despair.

In the Bible the apostle Paul warns against such mismatched marriages when he says, 'Do not be yoked together with unbelievers' (2 Corinthians 6:14). Such unions start with a handicap in the goal of creating a strong marriage for, Paul goes on, 'What does a believer have in common with an unbeliever?' They do have some things in common, of course, or else they wouldn't likely have married. But they don't share what's of central importance: love for Jesus Christ.

Anyone who has lived in such a marriage knows the challenges this represents. It can be terribly frustrating and lonely not to be able to share with your spouse the joy and fulfilment of knowing Christ. One woman (and it is most often the woman who is the believer) described her isolation as 'spiritual widowhood'.

There are almost certain to be clashes over finances: how to spend money and how much, if any, to give to the church. Will the children be raised to have faith or will the non-believing spouse oppose and undermine that? The non-believing spouse may even attempt to choke out the faith of the other. That can produce a lot of conflict and anger. And some women carry a heavy load of guilt over not being able to 'convert' their husbands.

It's not all bad news

But my experience is that the news is not all bad! No one living in an 'unequally yoked' marriage need settle for less than the best possible relationship. It's not easy. It takes commitment. But such a marriage can be strong and rewarding. Here are six guidelines that can help make it work.

1   COMMIT TO TRUSTING GOD

The principle that deepening your discipleship also strengthens your marriage applies to 'unequally yoked' marriages too. As your personal faith and relationship to God grows, it will inevitably have a positive impact on your marriage. Commit to growing your relationship to God and aim to live out your faith every day in your marriage.

When moments of pain, frustration, disappointment, even despair hit, remember that God wants to be your 'refuge and strength'. His loving eyes see your pain and his ears are attentive to your prayers. Let the Bible's promises and his Holy Spirit encourage you. You're not alone; God is with you.

2   COMMIT TO YOUR MARRIAGE

'… if a woman has a husband who is not a believer and he is willing to live with her, she must not divorce him,' says Paul (1

Corinthians 7:13). Commit to making your marriage as good and strong and rewarding (for both of you) as it can possibly be. Build on the common ground of your shared interests and hobbies, and focus on your areas of compatibility. Make your marriage as high a priority as you would if your spouse was a believer. Remember that the words of Jesus apply to 'mismatched' marriages also: '... what God has joined together, let man not separate' (Matthew 19:6).

3   COMMIT TO YOUR SPOUSE

In mismatched marriages, the believing spouse has many opportunities to practise the discipline of daily grace. Not only is your spouse not perfect, but it may be that as a non-believer, his or her imperfections are even more obvious to you. Here's where it's good to resolve to be a 'diamond miner', not a 'dirt farmer' in your marriage.

Keep your expectations realistic and focus on the positive in your spouse. Your spouse is not your project to fix; but your partner to love. It's not your responsibility to 'convert' anyone. Your spouse's spiritual decisions are between them and God. It's the role of the Holy Spirit to bring your spouse to faith. Yours is to love and honour. Even in mismatched marriages, every wife needs and deserves her husband's love; each husband needs and deserves his wife's respect. It's a biblical command that's both wise and practical (Ephesians 5:33).

Practise the discipline of daily grace by commiting to love your spouse with 1 Corinthians 13 love: love that is patient, kind, not self-seeking, not easily angered, keeps no record of wrongs, is always hopeful and never failing. Believer or not, your spouse is made in the image of God and greatly loved by him. Let your daily love and grace show that. Perhaps that love will draw your spouse to its author.

4   COMMIT TO YOUR CHILDREN

Discussions over raising the children are common to all marriages but can be especially heated when one spouse is not a believer. The unbeliever may fear that the children will be 'indoctrinated' or somehow turned against them. Or the unbeliever may simply not support your efforts to nurture faith in your children.

The soundest advice I can offer is my paraphrase of Moses' advice to Israelite parents in Deuteronomy 6:4–9: 'Be the person you want your children to become.' Be their model and teacher. They can't help but be shaped by it. If you are a believing wife with an unbelieving husband, use everyday situations in family life to build your children's faith – making sure to teach and model respect and honour, if not always agreement, for their father at all times.

5   COMMIT TO PRAYER

It's easy to fall into the the pit of despair over your spouse's unbelief and feel guilt over his or her unwillingness to convert. Thoughts that 'If only I'd… ' may haunt you. The result is often a constant state of disappointment with God and with your spouse. That makes it much harder to live in faith that God is still at work in your spouse and that you can have a strong, rewarding marriage.

That's why it's so important to pray – regularly, consistently and passionately. Pray for the love that comes hard some days. Pray for the grace to forgive. Pray for your spouse to come to faith. 'How do you know, wife, whether you will save your husband? Or how do you know, husband, whether you will save your wife?' writes Paul in 1 Corinthians 7:16.

6   COMMIT TO SEEKING SUPPORT

'Two are better than one … if one falls, his friend can help him up … ' (Ecclesiastes 4:9). Seek the support of at least one good Christian friend who can help you keep perspective during hard times and encourage you when you're down. And remember that the church is a family and is there to provide loving support, too.

Building survival skills 4: Growing a happy marriage

Any marriage requires work and discipline in order to be successful. Here are some tools to help you and your spouse check your progress as you grow your marriage.

1   What are some of the ways you currently practise each of the daily disciplines of marriage? Is there something you can add?

Keeping in touch

Ways I/we practise it now:

Way(s) I/we will add:

Daily grace

Ways I/we practise it now:

Way(s) I/we will add:

Growing together

Ways I/we practise it now:

Way(s) I/we will add:

Growing in faith

Ways I/we practise it now:

Way(s) I/we will add:

2   'As you deepen your discipleship, you strengthen your marriage.' What are some new ways you can put this principle into practice? (Don't skip this if you are in a 'mismatched' marriage!)

3   Evaluate your basic priorities: God first, then spouse, then children, then work. If they're not currently in the proper order, what will you do to correct that?

4   If you are in a 'mismatched' marriage, evaluate how and how well you are living out the six commitments given in the chapter. What specific commitments will you strengthen? What's your plan to do that?

5   'Love is patient; love is kind. It does not envy, it does not boast, it is not proud. It is not rude, it is not self-seeking, it is not easily angered, it keeps no record of wrongs' (1 Corinthians 13:4,5). Assess how your love for your spouse measures up to these standards. Identify areas of strength and weakness in how you express your love and note two or three steps that you can take to improve this week.

5 Surviving and thriving in single-parent and blended families

A COUPLE of decades ago the vast majority of families consisted of two parents and their biological children. But anyone who looks around their community today realises how much has changed.

Families now come in a variety of forms. There are single-parent and blended families (formed when parents bring their children from previous marriages into a new marriage). In fact, about 65 per cent of remarriages in the UK now include children from a previous relationship.

A single-parent or blended family was notable 40 years ago just because it was so rare, especially among Christians. But this is not the case today. For example, the number of lone-parent families in the UK in 2004 was approximately 2.5 million – an increase since 1996 of over 12 per cent. About one in four families in the UK is headed by a lone parent (usually the mother). And there are now 12 million single-parent families in the US.

Despite growing numbers, single-parent and blended families do face some unique and significant challenges if they are to survive and thrive. For some families, those challenges never seem to let up. As one single parent told me, 'After seven years we're still going from crisis to crisis'. But challenges don't have to be insurmountable obstacles, especially when met with courage, faith and determination. In fact, as I met and talked with single or step parents, I've seen how that's happening all the time, especially in families with faith.

Making peace with the past

The end of a marriage, whether by death or divorce, always represents a loss. It may be the loss of a beloved partner or the loss of the dream of love 'til death us do part'. The death of a relationship in which you have deeply invested is extremely painful and almost always involves at least one (and often both) of two powerful emotions: grief and guilt.

Everyone grieves in their own way and in their own time, but everyone *does* grieve. And it's important to take the time to allow yourself to grieve your loss. Grieving prepares us to bring closure to one part of our life so that we can move ahead, whether as a single parent or in a new relationship as part of a blended family. Look your losses squarely in the face, recognise the changes you'll face and count your blessings! Then you can make peace with your past and move on.

Let your children grieve, also. Whenever a parent is lost, whether by death or divorce, children mourn, too. Their dream of being a family forever has died too. Acknowledge their hurt. Let them talk about their sadness. And children often feel guilty that they're somehow responsible for the breakup of your marriage. So they'll need plenty of assurance that they aren't!

Forgive, forgive, forgive!

Perhaps you feel guilty too. Perhaps there are things you think you could or should have done to keep your marriage together. Perhaps you feel guilty about the pain you've caused your children or the trouble they're having adjusting to your new situation or marriage. Perhaps you don't even know *why* you feel guilty. And there's no way to pretend that some of the responsibility for the breakdown isn't yours.

In his book, *Seven Keys to a Healthy Blended Family*, Jim Smoke observes that forgiveness is vital to moving on and having healthy family relationships. He says that one of the biggest tools of destruction in families is unwillingness to forgive yourself and your former spouse for whatever was done to end the marriage: 'If you can't forgive, you can't live a healthy existence anywhere with anyone, whether in a blended family or with your children in a single-parent family.'

So accept your responsibility and any legitimate guilt. If you confess it to God, he will remember it no more (Jeremiah 31:34). God forgives and forgets – so we can too. Replace guilt with grace, recognising that you are greatly loved and treasured by God. You can be confident that nothing – not even a failed marriage – can separate you from God's love and care.

And extend that same forgiveness to your ex-spouse too. Forgiveness doesn't mean that no wrong was done to you; it means you will no longer let anger and bitterness control you. And remember that forgiving may not be 'once and for all'. If 'situations' continually arise with your ex-spouse, forgiving must be continual too. Forgiving yourself, your ex-spouse and, perhaps, the 'other woman' or 'other man' clears the emotional field so that it's more likely you won't carry the baggage of unfinished business and unresolved anger over into your new family situation.

> Do not judge, and you will not be judged. Do not condemn, and you will not be condemned. Forgive and you will be forgiven.
> *Luke 6:37*

Surviving and thriving as a single parent

Most people don't expect to be lone parents. But you may find that you are one – and wondering if you can make it alone. Here are five basic guidelines that may help.

1   GET CONTROL OF YOUR FINANCES

Many single parents look back on their first months and say something like, 'I really wish I had better control of my finances right from the start.' The standard of living of most single parents (most of whom are mothers) and their children often drops significantly after divorce or the death of a spouse. One advocacy group asserts that most two-parent households (with one child) have an income four to five times that of most lone parents.

Wise single parents move quickly to get control of the family's finances. Draw up a careful budget. Get a trusted, experienced friend to go over it with you. Will you need to work full-time? If so, what will you do for childcare? You'll need to investigate adequate and affordable caring arrangements and figure those costs into your budget. If you need affordable childcare or help in paying for it, you may be eligible for government assistance. And don't neglect to pursue child support if you are entitled to it.

In the UK, the Working Tax Credit can be worth up to 70 per cent of the childcare costs for a single parent working at least 16 hours a week. You may also be eligible for a childcare subsidy while receiving job training under the New Deal for Lone Parents (NDLP) programme. You may also qualify for income support. In England and Scotland, the Sure Start ChildCareLink is a government programme providing information on the availability of childcare. The DayCare Trust has a childcare information phone line too.

In the US, one of the best programmes for low income parents is the Women, Infant and Children (WIC) programme, which provides pregnant women and those with children under five years of age with nutritious food and referrals to health and social service agencies. It's available in all 50 states. US single parents may also qualify for food stamps to supplement their food budget. Some school districts have a Head Start or pre-kindergarten programme that provides both low cost childcare and nutritious meals for pre-school children. Many family advocacy groups provide single parents with advice as to how to seek these various benefits.

Realistic expectations are vital to successfully managing your finances. It's hard not to want to give your child everything she might have had if the family was still together. It's hard not to want to live the same way other families live. You may be tempted to give your children 'things' you really can't afford out of guilt for the pain they feel or the long hours you have to spend at work. But 'things' do not create healthy kids. Your loving, involved presence in their lives does.

And be creative with your housing arrangements! Housing can be one of the biggest drains on the family budget. It's no shame if you have to move in with your parents temporarily or perhaps share a flat with another single mum. Such arrangements may need to be very temporary and they won't suit everyone – but they might work for you.

2   GET CONTROL OF YOUR TIME
Single parents I've talked to say that one of the hardest things for them to do is to find time for themselves. But you can't be a good parent unless you take care of yourself. That means getting control of your time so that you can get adequate rest and exercise, prepare healthy meals and even have a little stress-relieving fun – meeting a friend for coffee, taking a hot bath with no interruptions or joining an evening class, for example.

Again, reality dictates that you won't be able to do everything you might have been able to do when you had the help of a spouse. You may not be able to attend every school activity or bake cakes for the kids' parties. Assess what you can do realistically and practise saying, 'No!' to the rest. Simplify your life in any way you can. Either you control your time or it will control you!

3   GET CONTROL OF YOUR EMOTIONS

We've already talked about the necessity of forgiveness; forgiving yourself and your ex-spouse. Anger and bitterness consume so much emotional energy that we have little left for our families. These emotions also undermine faith and hope in God. Forgiveness frees you from those negative effects so you can focus on your family.

It's easy to feel as if life has been unfair if you find yourself suddenly a lone parent struggling with financial and time pressures. But feeling sorry for yourself only drains you. It's more productive to trust in God's unfailing love for you; trust that he can work all things – even painful things – for your good.

Loneliness can be a major problem for many single parents. So it's no surprise if you're thinking about dating. But don't be in a hurry. Most counsellors advise single parents to re-enter the dating scene very slowly and carefully. One pastor who counsels singles at a large church in California says he believes it takes one year of healing for every four years of marriage. If you don't give yourself plenty of time to heal, you'll set yourself up for another fall.

Dr Kevin Lehman, in his book, *Single Parenting That Works,* says that when we bring a date into our children's lives we run a risk of hurting them greatly, should they become attached to your date but you decide to 'unattach'.

'If you want to raise healthy kids,' he says, 'waiting to date is the best thing you can do for them'. He advises waiting until the children are at least 18 and out of the house. Then date for a minimum of two years so you really get to know each other, and carefully introduce your children to your partner.

In the long run, he says, it's better to wait to date.

4 GET SUPPORT WHEREVER YOU CAN

I recently told one of my single parent friends, 'No one expects a single parent to be *super-parent*, so you shouldn't either.'

'You're wrong,' she told me. 'They expect you to be everywhere and do everything just as if you were in a two-parent household.'

Of course, that's neither fair nor realistic. Being a lone parent is hard. You'll need all the support you can get. And there *are* friends, family, people in your church, other lone parents and even government agencies ready and able to help. But they can't read your mind. Ask for help when you need it. And make it a priority to find one close friend you can share the ups and downs of life with.

One single mum told me how her supportive church introduced her to a Bible study and fellowship group with other single mums. The church also paid for professional counselling sessions to help her deal with guilt over her failed marriage, provided gifts of money from time to time, and had youth group leaders who took a special interest in her children.

The housebound mother with her first baby can feel acutely isolated, but single parents are particularly vulnerable. Many people say that when a relationship ends, they seem to lose friends as well as their partner, while the stress of bringing up children single-handedly can make it difficult for a social life.
Comment from Mind, the leading mental health charity in England and Wales

You may also find it helpful to join a support group specifically for single parents in your church or neighbourhood. In the UK, organisations such as Gingerbread and Single Parents UK sponsor support groups all over the country.

A word about divorced fathers

While it's true that most single parents are mothers, the number of single fathers is growing rapidly. In the US, the number of single fathers grew 25 per cent in a three-year period at the end of the '90s. Men now make up one out of every six single parents in the country. In the UK, single-father households are increasing by four per cent a year. These single fathers are struggling with many of the same issues that single mothers face and some very different ones also.

In the UK, government figures show that 650 children a day have parents who separate or divorce and 100 children each day lose contact with their father. Despite official government policy supporting 'shared residence' or joint custody, it's still usually the mother who is given primary or sole custody of the children when a marriage fails. Single fathers struggle to maintain regular and positive involvement in their children's lives, despite the fact that research shows conclusively that shared parenting is best for children.

A number of support and advocacy groups have sprung up in both the US and the UK to promote fathers' rights and shared parenting (joint custody), primarily by changing laws. In the UK, the most prominent group, until its recent disbanding, was Fathers4Justice. Its highly public demon-strations fixed attention on the frustration of fathers who have to apply to the courts to see their children. The Equal Parenting Council, which claims that joint custody is virtually never considered by judges, is also working to promote the rights of fathers to continue to be active parents after divorce.

The situation for divorced fathers in the US is somewhat better. Although the law varies from state to state, there is often a clearer presumption in law regarding joint custody. However, the activities of groups such as Fathers Rights US, Fathers Rights Inc and the American Coalition for Fathers and Children testify to the fact that many fathers face significant challenges gaining primary custody of their children.

5   GET TOGETHER WITH GOD!
There's nothing of higher priority for surviving and thriving as a single parent – or any other kind! – than attending to your spiritual life and health. You may not have a spouse, but you are not abandoned. You may not be married, but you are not alone. You can count on God's love for you.

So don't neglect regular worship at your local church. It renews your spirit and your hope. Take a few minutes each day for time alone with God, even if it's just ten or 15 minutes before the children get up. God wants to share your life and that relationship with him will be a continuing source of strength and hope. It will take some of your precious time, but it will be time well spent. And nurture the faith of your children too. Model for your children the person of faith you want them to become. Lead the way and expect your children to follow.

Surviving and thriving in blended families

Blended families are different from single-parent families in some ways, of course. But some of the challenges are similar. So it's no surprise their survival skills are somewhat similar.

1   TALK ABOUT FINANCES SOON
A blended family may have the advantage of two incomes but the two spouses may bring very different approaches to spending into the new marriage. That alone can produce a lot of heat in the family. In addition, the husband may be paying child maintenance to his first family as well as

supporting his blended family.

Some of the same financial solutions may apply here as with single-parent families: Child Tax Credit and Working Tax Credit in the UK can help with childcare costs. In the US, the Earned Income Tax Credit is a refundable federal income tax credit for low-income working individuals and families. The Temporary Assistance to Needy Families (TANF) programme can provide income support while a blended family gets on its feet financially.

Like the single-parent family, a blended family may have to adjust expectations and adopt a new lifestyle. It's best for the parents to recognise those changes at the beginning, agree on them and then share them with the children, perhaps at a family 'council' early in or just before the marriage. That way, everyone faces fewer unpleasant surprises!

Experience (and other spouses) tells me that communication is a key survival skill here. If possible, talk about your financial attitudes and values *before* marriage. As clearly as you can, face the financial issues and challenges *before* the marriage. Make a financial plan *before* the marriage. And *after* the marriage, keep talking, discussing, planning, compromising and working together too.

2   PREPARE WELL BUT DON'T HURRY!

Making two families into one big, happy family isn't easy. The lives of the children have been turned upside down. For them, divorce is the beginning of their problems, not the end. Now they have to get on with a new parent, new siblings and a new extended family of grandparents, aunts and uncles. It takes a calculator to work out how many new (and hopefully, harmonious) relationships need to be formed in this new family.

Each parent and each child comes to this new family with their own (sometimes conflicting) values, attitudes, traditions and memories. Also, the parents may have different attitudes and practices involving discipline and what they expect of the children. The family will be in permanent danger of being torn apart by an 'us and them' mentality unless all these differences are reconciled and owned by everyone.

All this 'blending' takes time, careful preparation and some struggle, as well as plenty of love. The problems many blended families face are often caused by not spending enough time discussing the changes they'll face and how each family member will adjust to them. So, if you're a parent contemplating forming a blended family, don't hurry. Give yourself plenty of time to heal from the wounds of your previous marriage. Plan lots of communication with your potential spouse and practise your listening skills! It may be helpful to get some professional counselling too.

Give your children and your potential spouse's children – especially if any are teens – time to get to know each other and build warm relationships. It might even be wise to move your new family into a totally new house – not one either family lived in before – so that no one has 'squatters' rights' and everyone starts out on an equal footing.

Some things can't be hurried. Some say it takes four to seven years for a blended family to feel comfortable. So don't hurry. Take your time and do it right!

3   GET CONTROL OF YOUR RELATIONSHIPS

If you ask them, most children would say they'd prefer to live in their original family. They had no choice about becoming part of a blended family and no say in choosing their step-parent or step-siblings. So it's no surprise if some children enter the new family feeling angry and disappointed. Some may even want to sabotage the new family situation. One of the biggest challenges blended families and single-parent families both face is managing these new, often strained, relationships.

Wise parents recognise that children need to love and be loved by both of their parents. So counsellors advise parents to facilitate as much as possible the relationship between the children and their non-custodial parent. It's not only that wise parents recognise that children need to love and be loved by both of their parents. A recent study of step-families confirms that frequent and satisfying contacts between children and the non-resident parent affects not only the quality of the relationship between the children and the resident parent but also the general happiness of the entire family.

So parents in strong families will try (as much as it's up to them) to keep on good terms with their ex-spouse (as well as their ex-spouse's new spouse!) and encourage their children to keep in touch with him or her as well. If physical contact isn't frequent, then this contact can be by phone, email or letters. And they'll even pray for the absent parent, both with the children and in private prayers. And, as hard as it is sometimes, they'll refuse to speak ill of the other parent in front of their children.

Oh the comfort, the inexpressible comfort of being safe with a person, having neither to weigh thoughts nor measure words, but pouring them all right out, just as they are, chaff and grain together; certain that a faithful hand will take and sift them, keep what is worth keeping and with a breath of kindness, blow the rest away.

Dinah Craik (1826–1887)

One stepfather said that accepting and avoiding criticising the biological dad in front of his children 'seemed to settle my step-children and cement in their minds that they were okay because their dad was okay.' Nor will wise parents use their children as 'spies' or as 'hostages' to get revenge over the non-custodial parent. Warm relationships with both of a child's parents are not only a gift to the child but, as studies show, a vital part of building a strong and happy family.

One important marker of the health of a blended family is the degree of marital satisfaction and personal happiness of the spouses. So one of the wisest recommendations I've seen for meeting the challenge of successfully blending two families is for both partners to go through pre-marital second marriage counselling. This will not only ensure that unresolved issues and problems from a previous marriage are addressed but help the couple do the work of blending their visions and expectations for this new, challenging family.

Despite what the Beatles' song says, love is not 'all you need' to make a successful blended family! But you can't have one without it; without the deep, unconditional loving commitment of each spouse to the other – the kind of love that is patient and kind, not self-seeking, not easily angered and which keeps no record of wrongs. Like God's love, it never fails – and no blended family can survive long without it. So spouses in healthy blended families make their marriage top priority and practise the daily disciplines of marriage covered in chapter 4.

The gift of this unconditional love and acceptance is one of the most important gifts spouses can give each other. It heals bruised and broken spirits and cements a relationship like little else. We all long for it and need it and, when we receive it, it comes as a true gift of grace from God. That kind of 'comfort of being safe', that 'breath of kindness', as one poet called it, provides the greatest insurance that marriages in blended families will be able to survive and thrive in spite of any challenges they face.

4   BUILD YOUR SUPPORT NETWORK

In light of all the challenges we've mentioned, it's clear that blending two families is not for the faint of heart! There will be days when you'll wonder if you'll ever stop being the 'bad guy' to your spouse's children, whether holidays will ever be really happy and uncomplicated, and if your blended family will ever feel like a 'real' family.

If you look around your community, you'll find plenty of other blended families. Many face the same challenges you do and most have developed the necessary skills to survive. So don't hesitate to learn from them. If you can find a blended family support group, join it. The best place to start is in your church, of course, so you can both share with other blended families and pray with them. If that doesn't work, advertise in your local newspaper and start a group yourself! Sharing your challenges and disappointments with others who really do know just how you feel can be just what you need.

And don't forget granny and grandpa! Actually, this advice applies to pretty much every chapter of this book. If you are fortunate to have a supportive grandparent (or uncle or aunt, for that matter) living nearby, then you have an invaluable asset to your family life!

Many grandparents are either retired or working part-time so it may be easier for them to spend quality time with their grandchildren. In a recent survey in the UK, 70 per cent of respondents said that being a grandparent was better than being a parent because they were free to enjoy the children without financial pressures. Three-quarters of grandparents are actively involved in their grandchildren's lives, especially where mum is working. Seventy per cent of employed women with dependent children use informal childcare – much of it provided by grandparents. Where grandparents provide such childcare, it's for an average of 15.9 hours per week – almost exclusively without payment, though in the UK grandparents can now be registered as childminders and get support and training in that role.

Unfortunately, grannies will not always be available!

Research suggests that more families live at greater distances to each other due to careers, divorce or separation. And more grandparents are continuing to work into the traditional retirement years. But, when they are around, as well as giving childcare, grandparents often assume the all-important role of confidant – a trusted source of advice and perspective, especially with teens experiencing some tensions with their parents.

5   NURTURE YOUR FAMILY'S SPIRITUAL FOCUS

One mother in a blended family said that in the early years of her new family, she 'learned to get real with God' as she brought to him her frustrations, disappointments and anger. Keeping an active prayer life is a key survival skill for your family. Pray and keep praying! Don't give up on God; he certainly won't give up on you. His love endures forever – and that's long enough to care for your family's needs. And the wonderful thing about God's love is that it is unconditional and self-sacrificial. Why else could God have sent his beloved Son for sinful people like us!

Thinking about discipline

I've purposely not talked about discipline, although that is one of the biggest challenges single parents and blended-family parents face. This topic is covered extensively in chapter 10. For now, it's enough to recognise that these general guidelines apply.

–   For blended families: Since each parent may bring their own – perhaps different – approaches to discipline to the new family, it's vital that they discuss and agree on their approaches to discipline. It's important to present a united front on discipline issues to the children, with each parent supporting the other in disciplining the children, especially when a child says, 'You're not my real mum/dad and you can't make me!' Divided discipline is no discipline.

–   For single parents: When you're exhausted after a long, hard day (or just feeling guilty for some reason), it's easy to let your discipline standards slip. It happens even in two-parent families. Instead of insisting that your child picks up her toys, you do it yourself. It may be easier in the short run but it's a recipe for disaster in the long term. Children need consistency in enforcing the rules. Inconsistent discipline is no discipline.

–   For both: Be patient. This new family is a big adjustment for everyone. Don't expect miracles, but do expect progress. And season your discipline with large amounts of love. Love 'covers over a multitude of sins' (1 Peter 4:8) and when discipline comes in the context of love that is patient and kind (in other words, like the love with which God disciplines us), it is much more effective in the long run.

Building survival skills 5: Surviving and thriving in single-parent and blended families

Single-parent and blended families face some real challenges, but every day they are meeting and overcoming them. These questions will help you identify and overcome your family's challenges.

1   How well have you made peace with your past, grieved your losses, dealt with your guilt and forgiven yourself and your ex-spouse? If you still need to do more in these areas, how can you move forward?

2   Identify the most pressing of the major challenges that your family faces. What first step will you (and, if applicable, your spouse) take this week to begin to meet them?

3   Identify the specific support networks (formal and informal) you have. Which do you still need or need to strengthen? What ideas do you have for accomplishing that?

4   How would you assess your personal relationship with God? Your family's spiritual health? What can you do now to begin to deepen your discipleship and strengthen your family?

5   How have you allowed God's wonderful forgiveness to impact the way you think about the difficult relationships you experience in your family?

SURVIVAL SKILL 3

Building a strong family faith

6   Nurturing your family's faith in the home

DRIVING HOME from work, Dad remembers. Tonight is the night each week his family lingers around the meal table for brief family devotions. He looked through the devotional booklet over the weekend, so he's prepared. It feels good to have the family together for this special worship time and he's convinced his family can't survive the many things working against their faith without this regular time together.

Then, just before the mealtime, the phone rings. 'Dad, I'm over at Jack's,' his teenage son says. 'They invited me to eat and, since I was coming over at seven for that study group meeting anyway, I think it's a good idea to stay. There's a big test in school tomorrow. I told you last week, remember?'

Dad doesn't remember, but he doesn't protest much either. It seems like his teenager is always finding some excuse to miss family devotions. 'We'll just have to go ahead without him,' he says to himself.

But when dinner time arrives, Mum hasn't arrived home yet. Traffic hold-up again! So Dad and his young daughter eat together. At least the two of them can share devotions together.

Just as Dad puts down his fork and reaches for the Bible, the doorbell rings.

'Can Emma come out to play?' a small voice asks.

'Please, Dad, I never get to play with my friends. Besides, it'll be dark soon and I'll have to do my homework.'

Dad takes a deep sigh and prepares for family devotions

alone. Sometimes he gets pretty discouraged. He wonders if it's really worth the effort.

Try, try – and fail again!

That fictional family and their struggles illustrate some of the challenges facing parents who want to have family devotions together. There are so many other activities – homework, time with friends, television, evening activities – all competing for those few, brief minutes. Individual schedules that seem too complicated and conflicting to allow for even a brief family time combine with disinterest from some family members to squeeze out family devotions.

One study estimates only five per cent of Christian families actually do have regular family devotions together. Most of the other 95 per cent are probably like yours and mine. They try and fail – and try and fail again, and only fitfully manage to have some family devotions before giving up in frustration and guilt!

What's the solution? Is the only alternative to resign ourselves to failure and give up? Some parents entrust the spiritual education of their children primarily to their church's Junior Church or even to a Christian school. In these settings, at least, there is regular time devoted to studying the Bible and worship. After all, the teachers are equipped and trained to do his kind of thing. Doesn't it make sense to let them do what they do best and, at the same time, relieve busy families of one more demand on their time?

No substitutes will do

Church programmes and Christian schools have their place, but there's no substitute for the home in shaping and nurturing the spiritual growth and faith of children. In fact, it seems clear that this has been God's intention from the beginning.

This was the core of what Moses, the great leader of Israel, told his people as they prepared to live as free families after their deliverance from slavery in Egypt. Moses told parents that he would teach them all of the principles, laws and decrees of God so that they and their children might revere and obey God as long as they lived. And, speaking on behalf of the Lord, Moses promised the people that, as long as they and their children did obey the Lord, they would be richly blessed (Deuteronomy 6:1–8).

But how would these parents carry out this important task? First, Moses told them to take all of God's commands 'to heart', to incorporate them into their own lives and then to 'impress' them on their children. Then, Moses gave the people specific examples of how to do that, and every example he gave has to do directly with everyday home and family life – where the most effective spiritual nurture of children takes place.

It's at home in the daily experiences of family life, Moses would say, that our children learn to know and love God and how to honour and obey him. This is the pattern in the New Testament period also. Entire families were sometimes converted to the new faith and then instructed in the faith together. This teaching often took place in the home, from house to house (Acts 20:20), as well as in the temple. The family grew in faith together this way, believing parents confident of raising believing children. This was the case with Paul's protégé Timothy, who had been taught the faith from his earliest days by his mother and grandmother (2 Timothy 1:5; 3:14,15).

> Where we love is home – home that our feet may leave, but not our hearts.
> *Oliver Wendell Holmes*

Values 'caught' at home

The first US presidential campaign I can remember was in

1960 when John F Kennedy beat Richard Nixon. I was only 12 years old, but I was a fervent Nixon supporter. Was my support based on my careful analysis of the relative positions of the two candidates? Hardly. Did it stem from a basic commitment to a particular political party? Not at all.

At 12 years old, my vocal support for Nixon was based only on one thing: the fact that my father, a long time Republican office holder, supported Nixon. I simply adopted my parents' political values as my own. I didn't understand *why* my father supported Nixon, but I knew he and our whole family did, so that became my attitude also.

This is, in fact, exactly the way children develop their earliest and most lasting values and attitudes. Children 'catch' their parents' values and attitudes on an entire range of life issues such as politics, relationships with neighbours, atti-tudes toward the poor and powerless, money and possessions, and racial matters. These early values and attitudes become a part of their very identity as members of their family.

Train a child in the way he should go,
And when he is old he will not turn from it.
Proverbs 22:6

So it is with spiritual values. The best way to nurture your children in a love for the Church is to love the Church yourself. Parents who practise the disciplines of regular, personal Bible study and prayer in the home, who make it a priority to be in church on Sunday, who demonstrate in their own lives a spirit of generosity toward those in need and reconciliation towards those with whom they have differences, will be much more likely to see their children incorporate those same traits into their own identities. These attitudes, values and disciplines will be part of what it means to be Pattersons or Joneses or whatever your family name is.

There are three basic practices to spiritual nurture in the

home which families might adopt: family devotions, the weekly 'family night' and what I call the 'family atmosphere' approach. We'll look at each separately.

Family devotions

One long-standing way of nurturing the faith of your children is with regular family devotions. It's easiest to start when your children are young so that it becomes a natural part of daily family life. Challenging as it is, with flexibility, creativity and perseverance, perhaps yours can be one of those select Christian families who successfully have regular family devotions. Here are six guidelines to help you get started.

1 FIND A REGULAR TIME

A regular time provides the benefit of an appointment that family members know about in advance and can plan for. It's not necessary that this regular time be daily, so long as it's a fixed part of your family's schedule. If you can't manage a daily time, try for a pattern of Monday, Wednesday and Friday or even just twice a week. If your weekday schedule is impossible, you may need to schedule some or all of your family devotions on weekends. That's okay – just schedule them! Mealtimes are often best, especially if you're able to have a regular family dinner time together. But, if mealtimes don't work, find another time.

2 BE CREATIVE AND HAVE FUN

Remember that the purpose of family devotions is not just to provide another opportunity for mum or dad to lecture. Some of that is necessary and good, but a steady diet will likely kill family devotions quickly. Set the goal of having everyone participate as much as possible. Ask the children to act out Bible stories once in a while. It will help keep them interested and involved so they learn more effectively. Let the children choose songs and lead them, too. Some will be able to read. Others may want to pray. Rotate leadership among family members as they are willing and able. And don't forget to have fun!

Be flexible enough to change what's planned if it seems a good idea. If one family member comes to the group with a special problem or question, that may be just the time to drop the prepared lesson and discuss how God and God's Word can help.

As a family you might wish to create a 'sacred' worship space, which might be the centre of the dinner table or a corner in the family or living room. In that space you might wish to place a cloth, or create a cloth from squares of people's favourite clothes that they have outgrown or worn out. You might wish to include a candle to remind you of the light of Christ, God's love made known. If you have a family Bible you might wish to place it open in this space and read parts of it when you gather at this 'sacred' worship space. Each member of the family might wish to include a small item that reminds them of God's love, or you might wish to decorate this space with seasonal items: like brightly coloured fall leaves; paper snowflakes; an Advent wreath; a crèche at Christmas time; gift boxes for Epiphany; sand to remind us of desert wanderings and testing for Lent; eggs as signs of new life at Easter; a kite at Pentecost; fresh flowers in the spring and summer; or a picture of your family and your church family if you have one. Use this space as a space to gather and share together in hearing and reflecting on the biblical story and on God's love for each of us that knows no bounds.

From an article on Family Devotions on the Belfast Cathedral website

3 USE THE TRIED AND TRUE *KISS* ('KEEP IT SHORT AND SIMPLE') METHOD

I heard two nursery-age kids arguing loudly one day. 'Jesus died for *me*,' one said.

'No, he died for *me*,' said the other. It made perfect sense to each that if the Sunday school teacher told them, 'Jesus died for you', that's what it meant – he died for 'me' and no one else!

Young children think very literally and concretely.

Doctrines such as 'vicarious atonement' (the understanding that Christ died in my place as payment for my sins) are very abstract and difficult for a child to understand – or many adults, for that matter. So be sensitive to the language you use in your family devotions, especially with the youngest children. Use material that is 'age appropriate'.

4   MAKE IT RELEVANT

How many times have you come away from church feeling frustrated: 'I spent 25 minutes listening to that sermon and heard absolutely nothing that I can apply in my life.' You knew you deserved – and needed – better. So do children. They experience that same frustration after listening to lessons that offer no answers to the questions they're asking.

You know what's going on in your children's lives; you know the problems they're facing. So try to show how the Word of God offers help, direction and encouragement. Help them see and marvel at how the Bible has something to say to four- or five-year-olds, or 10-year-olds or teens. It is very important to children that you demonstrate the *practicality* of Christianity to their life. If you don't, there is a danger that as they grow older they may reject the Christian faith as being irrelevant to their world.

Issues facing your family may also be the source of discussion sometimes. Or maybe you'll want to ask each family member to suggest one question he or she has about God's Word that the family can discuss. This helps keep our devotions in touch with the lives of our children as well as the wisdom of the Bible. Don't hesitate to share concrete, practical examples at work in your own life and faith. Your children will love them and learn from them too.

5   PREPARE IN ADVANCE

Family devotions need not require great blocks of time to

prepare (ten minutes may be adequate), but they do need *some* preparation – and that preparation includes prayer. If having more discussion during devotions is your goal, prepare one or two simple questions that can serve as discussion starters. Visit your local Christian bookshop or go to a Christian publisher's website to research good helpful materials. Don't limit your resources to the printed word – look at how you can use videos or CDs, music or craft to make your family time together more interesting and interactive.

6   DON'T FORGET TO PRAY

With young children, the prayer time during devotions shouldn't be long and involved. The language should be natural and simple. The most important thing is that you model prayer for your children. Encourage and invite – but don't force – your children to pray. Your devotions will almost always suggest a theme for prayer, but also ask the children if they have special concerns. Everyone should be able to ask for prayer for a concern of theirs and hear someone else in the family pray for it. You may want to keep a written journal of family prayers and a record of how God answers them; it's a great way to show your children that God *does* answer prayer.

The family night

In recent years, as regular family devotions have become harder to maintain under the increasing pressure of hectic schedules, a new practice has gained popularity: the weekly 'family night'.

What night of the week should you choose? Have you noticed that many restaurants and cinemas have special discounts on Monday and Tuesday evenings? Those are the nights of the week when people tend to go out the least. So, start there. Perhaps one of those nights will present fewer problems for getting the whole family together. Even the craziest family schedule will usually yield at least one night when everyone can be there. Like family devotions, make sure it's a fixed slot, so that when a potential conflict arises, family members know they have a prior commitment. Of course, be flexible. Activities such as school band concerts or work conferences are often scheduled far enough in advance so that, with planning, family nights can still be accommodated. As your children grow, family schedules change, so from time to time you may need to re-examine the best timing for your family night.

What should you do for family night? Since family nights are usually less frequent than family devotions, a family night can be longer. And two or three hours together one night a week is enough time to really do some fun and rewarding things together.

What about a special meal? Get the best dishes out and cook something together. After eating, have a time of Bible readings and prayers around the table. You might like to observe special times in the Church calendar such as Easter and Advent, as well as family birthdays and anniversaries. Some families play games or work on projects together.

For a while, when our boys were young, our weekly family time was on Mondays. By 7pm we had finished the meal and devotions and moved into the lounge to eat dessert as we watched our favourite TV programme. We really looked forward to this special time together.

Family atmosphere

'He's taking after his grandfather and you,' my wife said. She had just seen our teenage son give some money to his younger brother. There was no particular occasion that prompted this act; he just knew his younger brother would enjoy the extra money. So he gave it, just as his father and grandfather had done to him many times in the past.

The cliché is true: values are as much caught as taught. That's why what I call the 'family atmosphere' is so important a tool to parents who want to pass on their faith to their children. And every family has a family atmosphere, whether they're aware of it or not. It's made up of that big bundle of experiences that your family shares together every day: meals, homework, discussions (and arguments!), prayers, fun, illnesses, hugs – the list is endless.

Your family atmosphere is the emotional and spiritual soil in which your children grow and develop. If that soil is rich in love, kindness and spiritual sensitivity, your children have a head start at growing up to be self-confident, loving, kind and spiritually sensitive adults. If these nutrients are rare in your family atmosphere, your children's emotional and spiritual growth may be stunted.

Of the three different approaches to nurturing our children's faith – family devotions, family night and family atmosphere – each has much to offer. But the positive effects of regular family devotions or a weekly family night are greatly multiplied by a spiritually rich family atmosphere. After all, every day offers another opportunity to shape and mould your child's faith and character.

A combination of all three of these approaches would be tremendously powerful. But here's where I make my confession. We tried both family devotions and family nights. Each worked for a time and I'm glad we did them. I wish we could have been more successful, especially at regular devotions. But, as our family grew and changed, we came to rely almost exclusively on the family atmosphere approach.

'Watch my life'

The idea of the life-shaping power of the family atmosphere is at least as old as a story from the Bible I've mentioned before: Moses' instructions to the families of Israel as recorded in Deuteronomy 6. Moses begins by telling parents to develop their own relationship with God: 'Love the Lord *your* God with all *your* heart and with all *your* soul and with all *your* strength. These commandments that I give you today are to be upon *your* hearts' (Deuteronomy 6:5,6, emphasis mine). After being certain of their *own* relationship with the Lord, parents were told to teach God's commandments to their children so that they made a clear impression on their hearts. How was Moses to do this? No doubt, some formal teaching was involved, but it's not mentioned here. He didn't say, 'Be sure your children get to their classes in the faith education tent regularly' or even, 'Be sure you spend at least 15 minutes daily reading the Scriptures with them.' I'm sure Moses took it for granted that instruction in the faith would take place in some form in each family.

But what Moses *did* say indicates that the family atmosphere is the most essential, most fundamental area in which those parents could focus their efforts. 'Talk about [God's commandments] when you sit at home and when you walk along the road, when you lie down and when you get up,' Moses said (Deuteronomy 6:7). In other words, he advises parents to use the everyday experiences of family living to train their children in faith and godly living.

'Wasn't God good?'

My Dad was a dairy farmer all his life and, for as long as I can remember, he always (and I mean, *every day*) went out for breakfast after the morning chores. He'd shave, clean up and drive to a local coffee shop. It was part of his social life, and perhaps a reward for getting up at 3:45am each morning!

So when he and Mum came to visit us, Dad and I and my two sons went out for breakfast. I recall one particular Saturday morning that we drove a few miles to a local restaurant. Because it was foggy, I had put my car lights on. You guessed it! I left them on all through breakfast and, when we returned, the car battery was dead.

Neither Dad nor I were very mechanically inclined, but we knew there was *something* you could do with a standard transmission car to get it started. We just weren't sure what!

We were about to call my wife to come with the other car to rescue us when out of the restaurant came a man who offered to help us. He knew exactly what to do and, with one good push, the car started. As we drove out of the car park towards home, Dad said, 'Wasn't God good to send us that man to help us!' We all nodded in agreement.

'Wasn't God good…' How appropriate a thing to say right then! But, if Dad hadn't said it, we would have lost an opportunity to recognise and give thanks for God's care and involvement in our family's life. I was grateful to Dad for those words. They taught an important lesson to my sons, and to me as well.

Talk with your children about the things of God in the everyday experiences of life, Moses says. We should talk with our children about what is important to us when we're travelling in the car together, when we're working around the house, at mealtimes, at bedtimes – any time. When you're out together enjoying God's creation, when you hear about a neighbour who's sick, when you're talking about friends as you do the washing-up – take opportunities to talk together about matters of faith. This is the best way to help open their hearts and minds to see and experience God's presence and care all around them, every day.

Practising the presence of God

In the seventeenth century a monk named Brother Lawrence wrote a book called *The Practice of the Presence of God*. It has since become a classic of Christian literature. In it, Brother

Lawrence tells of his desire to sense God's presence in his life continuously throughout the day, whether he was cooking in the monastery kitchen or at prayer with the other monks. All times of the day and all activities of his life were to him the same: opportunities to commune with God, be in his presence and experience his care. He called this 'practising the presence of God'.

I believe that this should be our goal as Christian parents: that by our family atmosphere, we help our children practise the presence of God in their daily lives. When family finances are a problem, when someone is struggling at school, when someone is sick or a parent's job is especially stressful, the family can pray together. Such a prayer included with thanks before a meal or during bedtime prayers teaches that we believe God is present with us, cares about our situation and can be called on to help.

When those prayers are answered, don't forget to thank God. That teaches our children the proper response to God's presence and care. Just as we teach them good personal manners (to thank others), so we teach them 'good spiritual manners' too.

Without taking any time to plan or manufacture them, every family already has many experiences every day which parents can use to teach their children to reach out to Jesus and run to him at times of sorrow, pain or joy – or just out of love and thankfulness! Look out for those experiences and use them!

'I spy God'

So it's not hard to help our children practise the presence of God in their lives. The opportunities abound in daily family life. One family made a game of it; they called it 'I spy God'. As they discovered, when we purposefully look for signs of God's blessing in our lives, we will always find them. But, to be successful at this game, we may need to sharpen our own spiritual vision first. As we spend regular time with God in daily prayer, in reading his Word and in worship with others, our own eyes will be opened to see him with us. Then we can show him to our children.

If you're like me, you may need to be much more verbal about your faith in front of your children. For some of us, that doesn't come easy, but we must put aside our inhibitions. Our children need to hear us talk naturally about our relationship with Jesus and what he's doing in our lives. They need to see that their parents' relationship with Jesus is as real and important as the relationships they have with grandpa and grandma, with their friends and neighbours.

Children are great imitators. They learn so much by watching and then imitating – more formally called 'modelling'. If we say, for example, that the Bible is the most important book in the world, but they rarely see us reading it, what conclusion will they draw? If we tell them it's important to pray, but they never see us do it, what will they assume?

If, however, we let our children watch us as we recognise and respond to God's presence in our lives – just as my father did when the car battery was dead – they will learn to do it too. In a real sense, loving and following Jesus becomes as natural as loving and following mum and dad.

Tangible daily reminders

When my family lived in Pittsburgh, we lived in an older house in a predominantly Jewish section of the city. We soon discovered that every house on the block had a mezuzah on the door frame – a tiny cannister containing a miniature copy of the Torah, the first five books of the Old Testament. Referring to the things of God, Moses told parents to 'Tie them as symbols on your hands and bind them on your foreheads. Write them on the door-frames of your houses and on your gates' (Deuteronomy 6:8,9). The mezuzah on our doorframe was the way the Jewish people who lived there before us literally obeyed that command.

Here, again, Moses was talking about the family atmosphere. We don't need to take that command literally, but the principle behind it is still sound: put the things of God 'out front' in your home; make them a tangible, visible part of daily family life. That is one reason that Christian symbols, art and music have an important place in our homes. Together with the example we parents provide, they help to shape and reinforce the spiritual atmosphere of the home. They serve as reminders both to us and our children of who we are and what we believe as a family.

No time like the present

It's never too early or too late to begin enriching your family atmosphere to nurture your children's faith. We talked with our children about Jesus from their earliest days. Like many families, we sang lullabys such as *Jesus Loves the Little Children* and *Jesus Loves Me, This I Know* while we rocked and fed them. As they grew, it was natural for them to speak of Jesus, think about him and talk with him. A relationship with Christ is not just for adults. Surely the relationship of a child to Jesus will have to grow and develop as the child grows, but the fact that a child's relationship with Jesus may be immature does not mean it is not real.

If your children are older, don't let that stop you. God can still work great things in them as they see what he has done in you. If your children aren't born yet, it's not too early to begin. Work on deepening your own faith and relationship to God so that you children can 'taste and see that the Lord is good' (Psalm 34:8).

If you're someone who already practises a daily time of meeting God in Bible reading and prayer and weekly worship, you're already a long way down the road to creating a spiritually rich family atmosphere. If, on the other hand, you realise that you need to invest some time in yourself in order to enrich your family atmosphere, just start with what's manageable for you and grow as you can. Even a small, regular investment yields great returns for your family.

At the end of the book you'll find a list of useful resources I recommend for helping you in those personal devotion times.

Building survival skills 6: Nurturing your family's faith in the home

God has given parents the privilege of nurturing the faith of their children. Sometimes it seems like an overwhelming responsibility, but it needn't be. Use these questions to determine how well you're already doing and how to do even better!

1   How would you assess the strength of your family's faith? What obstacles make nurturing family faith difficult for you?

2   'These commandments that I give you today are to be upon your hearts. Impress them on your children. Talk about them when you sit at home and when you walk along the road, when you lie down and when you get up' (Deuteronomy 6:6,7). Identify two or three specific ways you can follow Moses' advice in your daily family life. How can you begin to practise them?

3   In two or three sentences, describe your 'family atmosphere'. What are you most pleased with? What do you want to improve? How will you do it?

4   What are some specific ways you can help your children practise the presence of God in your home?

7   Praying for your children

LIFE IS fragile. The world is a dangerous place. Temptations abound. Unhealthy influences surround us. So praying for their children is a key survival skill of families with faith. Believing parents pray for their children constantly, consistently and fervently. They begin praying for their children as early as possible, even before birth, and they never stop praying for them as long as either they or their children are alive!

When my sons were young, I felt the same anxieties and fears that many parents feel. How will my children turn out? Will they survive the rough and tumble of childhood? Will they grow up to follow Jesus as Lord? Will they be good caring friends to others? Will they have good marriages?

Since God has invited us to cast our cares on him (1 Peter 5:7), I decided to pray. From the day each of my sons was born, my goal has been to bring them to God – one father to another – daily. I know that, as fiercely as I love my sons, their heavenly Father loves them even more! I was present at their births but he, according to Psalm 139:13, created their inmost beings and knit them together in their mother's womb. So I knew that I could trust their lives and their futures to him.

Praying daily

Over the years, my daily prayers for my children have centred on their safety, their faith and their futures. Each day I pray for my sons, 'Father, you are their father and they are your children. Keep them safe today from sin and evil and harm. I trust in you and I trust them to you.' That simple prayer reminds me daily to trust my children to God and share with him the heavy burden of care for their safety. As one praying mother said of her children, 'When we release them to God, they are in good hands.'

As our children grow into young teens, they no longer look primarily to mum and dad for advice, values and opinions. Their friends have much greater influence. I found, as other parents have, that I didn't always like my children's friends or the influence they had on my sons. That caused me to pray that God would bring my sons good friends who would have a good influence on them. And I prayed for my sons' friends that God would give them, too, the gift of faith in Christ.

Also, as my sons became teens, I became more keenly aware of the tremendous sexual pressures young people today must face. Could they withstand them? Did they want to? So, in those years, my prayers took on an added request: 'Lord, they know what we've taught them. Please help them to want your best for them and somehow withstand the sexual pressures they face.'

Praying for their faith and their future

Of course, God alone is the one who gives the gift of faith in Christ. But he's assigned parents a role in the giving of that gift. It's never too early or too late to pray for your child to come to faith and to grow and mature in that faith. For many years, I prayed: 'Lord, remind my sons today who they are and whose they are. Let them know today that they are your greatly loved children. May they come to love and serve you by the grace of Jesus Christ.' As they grew, it sometimes seemed that God wasn't answering my prayers as fast as I'd like. But I just kept praying. What else could I do?

My prayers also reflected my belief that God had a good plan and purpose for my sons. And, as I thought about their futures, my prayers reflected that belief. As college approached, I prayed: 'Lord, fulfill your good purpose for my son. I trust you to take him to the right college.' And, after graduation: 'Lord, I trust you to provide a job, a flat, and lead him to a good church where he can grow in faith.'

Almost from their birth, my wife and I have also prayed for our sons' future wives. Since our sons are both still unmarried, we're still waiting for that prayer

> Making the decision to have a child is momentous. It is to decide forever to have your heart go walking around outside your body.
> *Elizabeth Stone*

to be answered. And, of course, we're still waiting for grandchildren. But I'm already praying for them, too; praying that they'll be born into a strong family where their parents will love them, love each other, and love Jesus Christ. So, even though my sons are grown, I've still got lots to pray about!

Praying with disappointment

Despite all their hopes, prayers and hard work, good Christian parents don't always produce good Christian children, at least not right away. Sooner or later, the time arrives when we can no longer control our children's choices.

God gives to them the same freedom to choose that he gave us. And some of their choices are foolish at best, sinful at worst.

> Ask and it will be given to you; seek and you will find; knock and the door will be *opened to you.*
> *Matthew 7:7*

When that happens, it's easy to feel pretty guilty. Where did we go wrong? Did God's promises fail somehow? Dare we still hope that our children will follow Christ in the end?

If you wrestle with those questions, you're in good company. Sinful though he was, the Old Testament King David was still 'a man after [God's] own heart' (Acts 13:22). His devotion to God – publicly and privately – was unquestioned. But his parenting skills were questionable. Take his son, Absalom. He refused to even visit his father for two years (2 Samuel 14:28). How that must have hurt and disappointed the great king! And, when Absalom finally did visit him, he began plotting to overthrow his father and soon drove him from the throne in fear and humiliation.

It's well known that evangelist Billy Graham's son Franklin led an openly rebellious life as a young man. His highly public, greatly respected parents must have felt hurt, regret and embarrassment; perhaps even guilt.

There's further encouragement for disappointed parents in Scripture in the parable of the lost son (Luke 15:11–32). Jesus told this story to give us a picture of the enduring, patient and gracious love of the Father for us – his prodigal (wasteful) children. The father in the parable was, no doubt, a wise and godly parent. Nevertheless, his son grew to be self-indulgent, immature and selfish. He demanded his share of his inheritance (not being willing to wait until his father's death), then ran away and squandered it all on sinful, shameful, dissolute living. What heartache and

Franklin Graham was a michievous boy who grew into a young rebel. He rode motorcycles, learned how to pilot planes and lived life in the fast lane.

'I just wanted to have fun,' Graham said, describing wild times of 'drinking beer, going out to parties and running around with different girlfriends.'

He smoked, drank, got into fights and admitted trying marijuana. He dropped out of one school and was expelled from another.

'He was behaving in ways that were not appropriate, to not only Billy Graham's son but to a young Christian,' said William Martin, Billy Graham's biographer.

One night in a hotel room in Jerusalem, Franklin's life changed. He says, 'That night instead of going to the bar for a couple of beers, I found myself alone in my room reading through the Gospel of John.

'When I came to the third chapter, I read not just that Jesus told Nicodemus he had to be born again, but I also grasped that Franklin Graham had to be born again as well.'

worry that son must have caused his father and mother!

Those parents must also have wrestled with guilt and disappointment; perhaps even disillusionment with God. Each day that the father waited and watched for his son to return must have been painful. But, in due time, the young man 'came to his senses'. He recognised the foolishness and sin of his chosen lifestyle and returned in repentance to his loving father.

By God's grace, that still happens today. Despite his early rebellion, Franklin Graham matured into the faithful and respected head of a reputable international ministry called Samaritan's Purse. Recently, he was officially chosen to succeed his father as head of his worldwide evangelistic ministry. How long, I wonder, did the Grahams pray for their son before God graciously answered?

Persisting in prayer

In strong Christian families where a child has strayed (or never seemed to be on the path at all), the parents continue to trust that God has a good purpose for their children and the children of all believers. Whether or not their children seem to have 'turned out' as their parents hoped, they continue to trust and pray that God will work in their grown children to fulfill his good purpose.

I trust God's promises and good purposes for my sons – but I keep praying. The parable of the persistent widow in Luke 18 is my model for prayer for my sons. This woman cried out day and night for justice; and disappointed parents can cry out to the Lord consistently and persistently, also. My own practice, in addition to praying for my sons daily, is to set aside a half-hour lunch break once each week to pray specifically and exclusively for them. In addition, from time to time, I've enlisted the prayers of a small group of family friends to pray for them regularly, too.

Faithful, not finished!

Parenting offers no guarantees except this: God is faithful. Despite its many demands, parenting can sharpen our prayer life, stretch our faith and force us to put our hope in God's enduring faithfulness, knowing that he is not yet finished with his good work in us or, thanks be to God, in our children. So faithful parents pray for their children as long as God gives them life. That's a survival skill no wise parent ever neglects!

Building survival skills 7: Praying for your children

God invites us to pray about anything – and nothing is more important to most parents than their children. Take some time now to check up on your discipline of praying for your children.

1   'Ask and it will be given to you; seek and you will find; knock and the door will be opened to you' (Matthew 7:7). Can you identify any obstacles which prevent you from a regular commitment to praying for your children?

2   If you don't yet pray regularly for your children, make a pledge and a plan to begin this week. Identify the time, place and frequency of your prayers for them.

3   Make a list of the specific areas you'll pray about regarding each of your children. You may want to include safety, their future (education, job, friends, spouse, etc), and faith development as well as any other specific concerns.

4   If you are praying with disappointment (or even anxiety), what will encourage you to keep praying? What can you learn from the parable of the lost son (Luke 15:11–32), for example?

5   Is there someone who could be your prayer partner; someone who can support you and hold you accountable to pray regularly? Identify that person. Plan to ask him or her.

SURVIVAL SKILL 4

Celebrating everyday family life

8 Making family memories: rituals and traditions

FOR SOME of us, talk of family rituals and traditions brings to mind dull, painfully boring family activities; things everyone *had* to do but no one ever enjoyed. Perhaps it was the long holiday visit at great-grandmother's house when the parents spent all their time trying to keep the children from breaking everything, while the children spent all their time fighting frustration, boredom and each other!

For others, however, talk of traditions and rituals evokes very different memories. They remember the fun of decorating the Christmas tree together or the special birthday meal which meant you could choose anything you wanted – even all desserts! Or simpler things like bedtime stories and prayers.

Good memories or bad, those family rituals and traditions are part of us forever. We often go to great pains to share the special ones with our own children, to share with them that same warmth and specialness those family rituals and traditions gave us. And, as we do, we experience the great benefits of family rituals and traditions: they help us celebrate everyday family life while building family faith, identity and belonging. They are vital to families that survive and thrive!

> Every day of our lives we make deposits in the memory banks of our children.
>
> *Charles R Swindoll in The Strong Family*

Routine or ritual?

Much of what we do in the home every day – getting up, eating, sleeping, doing chores – is just routine. These are things we need to 'get over with' so that we can get on with our own individual agendas, the real business of living such as work, college etc. The many demands on our time mean that, if we're not careful, the rituals and traditions we so value will be gradually squeezed out of family life.

So what's the answer? Psychologist Dr Paul Pearsall, author of *The Power of The Family*, recommends consciously seeing much of what we do as a family not as a routine or chore but as an opportunity for family ritual. But what's the difference between routine and ritual? We tackle routines without a great deal of thought, wanting to get through them quickly. In contrast, rituals are the things we go about with some sense of ceremony, slowly and thoughtfully. They force us to slow down a bit.

In the classic musical *Fiddler on the Roof*, Tevye, a peasant living in a small village in pre-Revolutionary Russia, is faced with the challenge of maintaining family and religious traditions while adjusting to political and societal changes. Tevye explains that he and others in his village have followed the same traditions for many years – and that it is because of their traditions that each of them knows who they are and how they are expected to live. 'Without our traditions,' he comments, 'our lives would be as shaky as ... a fiddler on the roof!'

Bedtime preparations, sharing reports of the day around the dinner table, family prayers and doing chores together all can become family rituals that demonstrate the shared belief that *even ordinary family activities have meaning and significance*. They transform our family routines (dare I say, even *redeem* them) allowing us really to experience and celebrate family living within the daily routines of our busy families.

Even simple acts such as holding hands around the dinner table to pray before meals become rituals which strengthen family ties. In contrast to family routines, family rituals celebrate family togetherness, focusing intentionally on sharing and enjoying the many things families do together, allowing us to slow down and 'smell the roses'. They are important precisely because they are done together, shared and savoured slowly, rather than done individually and hurriedly.

A sense of belonging

Do you remember ever having your own club when you were a child? I can remember at least two that I invented and belonged to. Children love to have a sense of belonging to a unique group that is somehow distinguishable from all others. The first and most important club they need to feel they belong to is, of course, their family. It's the one place where, as the poet Robert Frost put it, 'when you have to go there, they have to take you in'.

Families that do take time to build rituals and traditions regard them as necessities not frills. In return, they are rewarded with a strong sense of connection. But if a family is 'under-ritualised' – caught up in just getting through life instead of celebrating and sharing life together – there is danger that the children will be unable to feel that sense of real belonging to the family they so want and need. They may begin to look elsewhere to find a 'family' to belong to. That 'elsewhere' may turn out to be an unhealthy peer group or gang.

Paul Pearsall's research with adolescent boys who joined gangs indicates that such boys usually come from homes lacking a system of family rituals. Gang rituals become substitutes for family rituals, giving their lives some signficance, order and meaning. He even points to drug and alcohol misuse – behaviour which seems to mock the value of life itself – as symptoms of lack of ritual. Such activities as having pancakes on Saturday mornings or praying together the night before a child's exams give security, stability and meaning to our children in the midst of an unpredicable world.

A sense of family identity

Traditions shape our identity and give us a sense of place in relationship to others. Each family needs its own traditions. Some of ours are quite simple: renting a DVD on a Friday night, spending Thanksgiving at the grandparents', Advent calendars, or going together to the Christmas Eve watch-night service. Not only do such traditions foster in us a sense of belonging but they give us a way to define who we are as a family: 'This is what the Pattersons do.'

Family reunions are another tradition that often very effectively affirms family identity. They help pass along family history and a sense of continuity. As well as smaller get-togethers, the Patterson family holds a major reunion every summer near the dairy farm where I grew up. Anywhere from 55 to 75 people come, at all ages and stages of life, and some from a great distance. As you can imagine, it's quite an experience! We gather for a whole day at a park. We mostly eat and talk – there's quite a bit of both! My wife, sons and I try to attend each year if at all possible. It's the only time we see some of those aunts, uncles and cousins, and I want my children to know them as real people, not just names on a Christmas card.

> But you are a chosen people, a royal priesthood, a holy nation, a people belonging to God, that you may declare the praises of him who called out out of darkness into his wonderful light.
> *1 Peter 2:9*

Family holidays

Family holidays are another great way to build a sense of family identity and belonging. They provide a special time and place to be together and do things together that the family has planned and anticipated all year long. In other words, they offer times to establish and carry on traditions.

For over 25 years we have taken our family holiday on Nantucket, a small and beautiful gem of an island far off the coast of Massachusetts. In fact, 'Nantucket in August' is one of our more popular family traditions. We enjoy going to the beach together, exploring the island and going into the lovely little town in the evening.

While we're there, we have plenty of time to do things on our own, but we spend a lot of relaxed time together too. Our vacation gives us a time and place to nourish and celebrate our love and closeness as a family.

Christmas and Easter

Events in the Church calendar offer parents opportunities each year to teach spiritual truth through establishing holiday traditions. The two great holidays of the Christian faith, Christmas and Easter, are especially helpful. Here are just a few brief ideas for holiday traditions that may kindle your own creativity.

- Nativity scenes: Our family used them as soon as our children were old enough to play with them safely. Let the children handle and play with the figures while you tell the story of the birth of the Christ-child.
- Advent calendars: If you can find one, buy one with windows that contain a Bible verse or two. Let the children open one window each day, perhaps at the evening meal. As they are able, they can read the verses and listen to your explanation.

- Christmas presents: Encourage family members to make gifts that communicate real thoughtfulness and love. Be creative! Maybe the gift will be something handmade or sewn or a voucher for doing the other person's chores.
- The Jesus Box: During Advent, each family member puts in loose change. On Christmas Eve, the money is donated to the church or used to help a needy family. One Christmas, our family bought vouchers to use at the local grocery store for a family in need.
- Coloured Easter Eggs: One family I know colours hardboiled eggs in bright colours in celebration of the joy of Easter, leaving one egg white to signify Christ's sacrifice to make us sinless and forgiven by God.

Linking faith and family

When you think of some of the traditions your family observes that express your faith, what comes to mind? Grace before meals? A family night or devotion time? Serving meals for the homeless? Regular attendance at worship? Celebrating the great feasts of the Church year? These rituals identify us as families committed to honouring Christ. They are also clear symbols of our faith which communicate powerfully, clearly and non-verbally to our children and are an important part of our 'family atmosphere'.

Faith is rarely passed on if it is just about theology and doesn't make a difference in daily life – and rituals and traditions are one of the best ways of experiencing that difference.

My wife and I wanted to communicate to our children the value of serving the poor. But we live in a comfortable middle class neighbourhood and our children went to a nice, suburban school. So we struggled with how to help our children develop and maintain a heart of caring and service to those in need. We stumbled on a way to do it almost by accident. My wife took a teaching position at an inner city school just two blocks from the City Mission. When she heard that the Mission needed volunteers to help serve a meal on Christmas Day, we signed up as a family to help. Quickly, 'Christmas at the City Mission' became a Patterson family tradition. It's a tradition that helped keep us in touch with the needs of others and allowed us to serve them together, as followers of Christ. It's a tradition I'd be pleased to have my children pass on to their children too.

Celebrating the special within the ordinary

Family life is mostly lived in that vast expanse of time we call 'everyday', not just in the great faith festivals. And there are many wonderful family traditions that celebrate our faith without any link to any holiday or Christian festival. Such traditions enable us, as in the examples that follow, to celebrate the special within the ordinary of daily family living.

For as long as their children were at home, one family observed the tradition of celebrating family milestones such as the baptismal anniversary of each of their children as well as their birthdays. This tradition could be adopted to celebrate a confirmation date or the date of profession of faith. And why not a family celebration for passing the driving test? Or to mark graduations?

When our younger son graduated from high school, we asked various older friends and relatives to write him a letter giving him sound spiritual advice and celebrating his many good qualities, his growth in character and his talents.

We've already seen how the daily routine of a young child's bedtime can become a very affirming and comforting ritual. A warm bath, a Bible story, bedtime prayers and a goodnight kiss can lift the transition from waking time to sleep (with all the fears of what will happen when the lights go out and mum and dad leave) out of the routine and ordinary and into the special. It is a ritual that celebrates this ordinary daily transition of family life exactly by making it a special daily reminder of the love, security and stability of the child's family.

What about the daily transition of leaving our children at their place of daycare? No matter how prepared we or our children are, when it's time for mum or dad to leave, the child's cries are enough to turn a statue to tears! Many parents have found that rituals help smooth this transition. Some do it with a discussion of the child's activities in the day ahead: 'Tell me what you think you'll do today' or 'Let's see if I can guess what you'll do today at nursery … I'll be thinking of you when you're doing those things. I'll probably be doing… Will you try to think about me, too?' Then, a hug and a kiss mark the end of the ritual.

A 2004 report claims that children aren't getting enough sleep – or enough bedtime stories. One in five youngsters gets two to five hours a night less sleep than their parents did at their age. TVs, computers and electronic games in children's bedrooms are largely to blame, giving the children too much stimulus in contrast to the traditional bedtime ritual of a bath, warm drink and a story. The report, by Oxford University's Child and Adolescent Psychiatry unit, said that lack of sleep put at risk children's mental and physical health and academic achievements.

One family, whose children are a bit older, practise a daily 'ritual of leaving'. When dropping off the children at school (or when they leave the house to catch the bus), the mother makes the sign of the cross on the child's forehead and says a blessing such as: 'Go with God. Serve him well' or 'Remember, you belong to God'. The children can also offer a similar blessing to the parents.

Special family times

Most of the time, family mealtimes are about as ordinary as you can get! Holding hands around the table as you pray before eating, having each member tell one thing special (good or bad) about their day, or a 'God sighting' that day make an ordinary mealtime special!

Some families schedule a monthly 'date' between each parent and child. It might be nothing more than a trip to the cinema or the local fast food restaurant or spending a couple of hours at the museum, but they do it regularly and they do it together. Another family celebrates 'Brothers' Day' and 'Sisters' Day' on two Sundays between Mother's Day and Father's Day, when the children of the appropriate gender get to plan the menu and go on an outing with their parents.

The year is full of opportunities to start new traditions; even such apparently insignificant dates as the first and last days of the school year or the cat's birthday are opportunities to celebrate being a family. Look for those opportunities and celebrate!

Traditions for single parents

Single parents need to develop their own special traditions and rituals to help them meet the special challenges of lone parenting. For example, now that her kids are old enough to manage downstairs without her for a short time, one single mother has a nightly ritual of 30 minutes alone in the bath after work to soak, relax and enjoy the quiet. Only after being renewed by this nightly ritual does she begin preparing dinner. Another working single mum, who always felt exhausted by the time her child went to bed, invented 'good morning stories'. Just before bed, she and her son pick out a book to read in the morning, after they are dressed.

Some single parents get together to celebrate Mother's

Day. One group of four established their own tradition of a Mother's Day Brunch. They draw names to buy presents for each other and help each other's children buy presents too. When the day arrives, they hire a sitter for their children and enjoy a pleasant brunch while opening their presents. Pretty creative, isn't it?

Growing seeds of hope

Rituals and traditions help our families sink roots deep in the soil of closeness and intimacy while lifting our spirits to have confidence in the future ahead. They create memories that endure – and help our families endure – for a lifetime.

In these memories, as family specialist Dolores Curran has observed, grow the seeds of hope. Hope is based in memory, and family traditions and rituals build hope through creating memories. That hope, in turn, sustains us as we travel from yesterday into today and it gives us the courage we need to face tomorrow.

So what better time can we spend with our family than that which builds hope and faith and love? These three things – like our family rituals and traditions – endure forever (1 Corinthians 13:13).

Building survival skills 8: Making family memories: rituals and traditions

Rituals and traditions make memories, grow hope and bind families together in many wonderful ways. Use them to help your family survive and thrive!

1   List two or three of your favourite childhood family rituals or traditions. How have you passed them on to your children?

2   'But you are a chosen people, a royal priesthood, a holy nation, a people belonging to God, that you may declare the praises of him who called you out of darkness into his wonderful light' (1 Peter 2:9). How would your children describe who they are; their identity? Do they see themselves as 'people belonging to God'?

3   What family routines does your family have that could become family rituals or faith rituals? Identify them and briefly describe how you might make the change.

4   What are some ways your family does or could celebrate the special in the ordinary?

9 Having fun is serious business

IN HIS book, *The Effective Father,* Gordon MacDonald tells how Boswell, the biographer of Samuel Johnson, referred to a special day in his childhood when his father took him fishing. Even as an adult, Boswell remembered that fishing trip vividly. It must have been a thoroughly enjoyable experience for the young boy.

MacDonald says that because Boswell mentioned that fishing trip so often, someone decided to check the journal Boswell's father kept in order to see what he had thought of that day. Under that date, the journal entry had only one sentence: 'Gone fishing today with my son; a day wasted.'

'A day wasted.' What a sad reflection! Which of us has a day (or even a few hours) to 'waste'? Supporting our family, pursuing our career and raising our children don't allow for any time to waste.

As a result, we're often too busy to have fun with our families! It's not easy to shake the belief – rooted, as we saw, in the job culture – that work is what is really significant in life. On the other hand, fun can seem not only frivolous but expensive too. We have neither time nor money to waste on either fun or frivolity. Better just to keep to the really important, serious aspects of family life.

> Therefore I tell you, do not worry about your life, what you will eat or drink; or about your body, what you will wear. Is not life more important than food, and the body more important than clothes?
> *Matthew 6:25*

Let me say it as clearly as I can: having fun together as a

family *is* important. It *is* serious. Family fun returns great rewards to the family that invests even small amounts of time in it. Having fun together is a key survival skill of families today.

The case for fun

Adults, as well as children, need to relax, play and have fun. By refreshing our spirits and renewing our bodies, play and fun become true sources of 're-creation' for our lives. For young children, play *is* work. Through play, they work out their understanding of life; how to cooperate, how to get along with others, how to win and lose graciously. Through play, they learn to cope with their fears and worries of the past and present. There is so much we can help them learn just by playing and having fun alongside them while sharing our insights and offering our example.

Relieving stress

Is your child taking a test in school this week? Is he entered in a competition soon? Is she new to the school and still trying to make new friends and fit in? If any of these apply to your child, he or she needs to play and have fun (with you and with other children) for another good reason: stress relief.

Some children are under a great deal of stress today. Family turmoil, heavy academic pressures, peer pressure... These and other stresses, which I discuss in my book *Brand-Name Kids: The loss of childhood in America,* weigh heavily on children today. The result is often restless, irritable children who may be tense or even seriously depressed. They need help to recover a healthy, balanced life. They need the time and the permission of their parents to play and have fun.

Fun activities such as playing a board game with our children – and letting them win – or getting down on the floor to wrestle with them gives them that time and permission to put the fun back into their stressful lives.

Play builds self-esteem

Although Boswell's father didn't realise it, that 'wasted day' fishing stayed with his son for a lifetime. How important that boy must have felt having his dad all to himself for that entire day. Taking time to play with our kids gives a big boost to their self-esteem.

Now a word of caution. If we play with our children for the sheer pleasure of being with them, everyone benefits. If, however, our body is there but our heart and mind are somewhere else, nobody benefits. That really is wasted time.

Making family memories

Another reward of family fun time are the memories it makes. When our children were young we made it a tradition to go camping together one weekend in the spring and one in the autumn. One year we went in a borrowed tent. It rained the whole first night and the tent leaked liberally! We woke up lying in a big pool of water. The rain continued the whole of the next day, so late in the afternoon we gave up and went home. We still laugh about it; it's quite a family memory.

Playing together ... helps build strong bonds between parents and children. When there is a strong parent-child bond, children feel safe to go out and explore the world. This makes them better prepared to learn, get along with others and develop high self-esteem. Children who feel secure in their relationship to their parents also do better in school.

Another reason that play is important to parent-child bonding is that it helps increase the number of positive interactions in the relationship. Often, the only times parents talk to their children is when the children have done something wrong. When this happens, children and parents can stop getting along well and may not develop strong bonds.

Kathy Gould of the support website
www.practicalparent.org.uk

The family that plays together...

As we've discussed, time and money are at a premium for many of us with families, particularly if we're single parents or are raising blended families. So how can we find time to have fun together? Let's look at seven guidelines.

1   DON'T BE AFRAID TO HAVE FUN

Perhaps surprisingly, the biggest obstacle to having fun together as a family is fear. We're afraid, like Boswell's father, that we'll waste our time, money or energy. But you can have family fun without that guilt! Research confirms what our common sense tells us. Healthy families have a sense of humour, fun and play. So don't be afraid to put aside your work from time to time and do something fun with your family. And don't make the mistake of turning play into work. Some of us tend to work hard even when we play. Remember the object of family fun time is enjoyment and relaxation.

2   DON'T BE PUT OFF BY THE EXPENSE

Family fun time doesn't have to be expensive. If your income is limited, having fun may require a bit more creativity. Ball games in the park, board games at the kitchen table, a walk around the neighbourhood, reading together or a trip out for an ice cream can be a lot of fun. When our boys were young, it seems as if we went to the local city museum about once a month, where the big attraction was the dinosaur exhibit. We also regularly used the indoor pool at a local school.

3   BE SPONTANEOUS

After all, that's the way your children are naturally! We adults tend to suppress our spontaneity. Unpredictability upsets our schedules. But children love it! So, sometimes, just drop everything and head out for pizza or drop in on a friend. Surprise the children with a torchlight hike around the area an hour or so before bedtime. Or put on a CD and dance in the living room. Your children will love it.

A spur of the moment weekend family picnic also makes a great outing. Throw together a few sandwiches, drinks and crisps, head to the park and take along a frisbee. Some parks have nature trails for exploring or hiking too.

4   PLAN TO HAVE FUN
In the light of our crowded schedules, there are limited possibilities for family fun time. If you know it's not going to happen any other way, schedule fun in your diary; actually write it on your calendar.

One way that I planned for those more time-consuming family activities such as camping trips was to mark on my calendar the time when my children didn't have school and then keep some of those slots free of my own commitments. If someone did ask me to do something else on one of those days, I could answer truthfully, 'I'm sorry, but I already have a commitment.'

5   INCLUDE YOUR CHILDREN IN YOUR DAY
A friend of mine recalls that when he was a child his father always seemed to be busy at something, even when he was not at work. He enjoyed building and repairing things around the house and was often in his shed busy on some project. It would have been easy for that father to get so caught up in what he was doing that he'd give his son the impression that any question or request to help his dad was 'bothering' him. Sometimes the thing a parent least wants to hear is a little voice saying, 'Daddy, can I help?' because you know your task will take three times as long with that kind of help!

But my friend remembers that his father was never too busy to find *some* way to include his son in his projects. So it's no surprise that some of my friend's best childhood memories are of just those fun times in the shed working with his father.

Young children love to participate in adult activities. They love to help. So, if you have to clear out the garage, do some gardening, go to the post office or hang out the washing, take time to include your children. The older they get, the more creative you have to be to involve them (teens, for example, are often *allergic* to work) but the younger ones are often proud to help.

6   MAKE FUN A FAMILY PRIORITY
Fun is essential to a balanced, healthy family life. And helping our children develop healthy patterns of recreation is one important thing we can do to ensure their future physical, emotional and spiritual health. Set an example for your children. Express enjoyment in the outdoors, find pleasure in reading together, or enjoy working on shared projects. Let your children see you put aside your work from time to time and just have fun with them.

Try to find at least one sport or hobby that everyone in the family enjoys so that you can do it together. When I was a child, our family sport was bowling and we bowled together almost every Friday night during the season. Usually, we went with another family or two so that there were other children the same ages as ours there too. Our family also enjoys what we call 'exploring'. I hasten to add that this does not mean anything so daunting as navigating wilderness rivers or underground caves! For us, it usually means driving an hour or so to a town or area we haven't visited before.

Perhaps you and your family would enjoy visiting a local nursing home once a month or helping at a drop-in for the disabled? For some families, these are not only service projects that strengthen and make visible their faith, but activities they genuinely enjoy doing together. With some thought and creativity, you can find at least one activity that you all enjoy and can do together. Then… do it!

7   HAVE FUN IN YOUR FAITH

Do the words 'faith' and 'fun' sound contradictory to you? Unfortunately, our children's most formative impressions of following Christ are often limited to those they receive in church, where the mood is often sober, voices are low and fun seems out of place.

Our children have a right to know that it's okay – good even – for Christians to laugh and have fun. God is not upset when we take a break from work; he did just that after he finished the creation. He's not upset when we do nothing more than have fun together and enjoy each other. After all, Jesus' first miracle was to change water into wine at a wedding party!

So look for ways to laugh and enjoy each other consciously as Christians, perhaps within your church fellowship. It's good for you and it's a great lesson for your children too. For strong, healthy families, fun really is serious business!

Building survival skills 9: Having fun is serious business

Family fun is often the first casualty in our busy, time-starved lives. But it offers so much to our families! Use the questions below to help you get started really having fun together!

1   What words or phrases best characterise your family's attitude to family fun? Would they include, for example, 'We're too busy' or 'It costs too much'?

2   'Therefore I tell you, do not worry about your life, what you will eat or drink; or about your body, what you will wear. Is not life more important than food, and the body more important than clothes?' (Matthew 6:25). If your family is too busy for family fun, try to identify the reasons or anxieties behind that. What priorities need to change?

3   List some of the major benefits for your family that you anticipate as a result of intentionally spending family fun time together.

4   List some activities that might well be enjoyable for the whole family.

5   What is at least one new way your family can have fun together this week?

SURVIVAL SKILL 5

Thinking positive about discipline

10 Disciplining is discipling

THE TERRIBLE twos… toilet training… sibling rivalry… adolescence. What do these all have in common? They all evoke negative images of discipline struggles and tensions between parents and children.

I see it in the faces and hear it in the questions of the many parents to whom I speak each year. There's no other topic that evokes such anxiety among them as discipline.

- 'It's a battle every day.'
- 'I have to watch him every minute.'
- 'We've got to show them who's in charge.'

Child development expert Dr Penelope Leach once asked 25 parents to describe a good disciplinarian. Nineteen of them said something like, 'Someone who gives clear orders and punishes consistently if a child disobeys'. Seen in these terms, is it any wonder that discipline is such a negative, unpleasant topic for parents and children alike?

But it shouldn't be. Of course, there'll always be children who want to assert their growing independence or just want what they want when they want it. But discipline is not all dark and dreary. It doesn't have to be an 18-year-long battle. Understanding that and how it works out in daily family life is a key survival skill for all families with faith.

What discipline is and isn't

There's more to discipline than just telling children what to do and punishing them when they don't do it. In fact, there is an important distinction between discipline and punishment.

They are essentially quite different: one positive, the other negative.

Discipline refers to the education and nurture of children, the cultivation of their mental and moral faculties. It is primarily educational, not punitive. It involves corrective measures to help eliminate undesirable behaviour and encourage that which is good. Whatever tools of discipline you use, the intent should be to help children identify the right and resist the wrong and unwise, rather than just to punish.

Punishment is basically negative. Its purpose is to hurt, to inflict pain. It rarely has a positive, restorative or redemptive goal. It may temporarily curtail the wrong, but doesn't teach the right. It doesn't instruct; it doesn't correct; it doesn't train; it doesn't encourage.

Discipline is basically training. In biblical terms, it is 'training in righteousness' (2 Timothy 3:16). It is gracious, yet firm. It looks forward to future growth rather than focusing on past failures. In that way, it encourages a child to want to do better the next time. Focusing on past failures only discourages. Punishment says, 'You failed again. You're rubbish.' Discipline says, 'That wasn't a good choice. You may have to bear some consequences. But how can you do better the next time?'

As Penelope Leach says, discipline is all about 'helping children grow into people who will one day do as they

> To smack or not to smack? Studies have shown that physical punishment, such as hitting, slapping and verbal abuse, are not effective. While such punishment may seem to get fast results, in the long term it is more harmful than helpful. Physical punishment can discourage and embarrass children and develop low self-esteem in them. Some experts argue that it also promotes physical aggression in children by showing them that violence is acceptable and that 'might makes right'.
>
> *From guidelines produced by the National PTA of the US.*

should and behave as they ought when there's nobody around to tell, supervise or punish them.' When you look at discipline that way, it really is much more positive.

What's your goal?

Have you clearly defined what you want your children to be like when they grow up and how you can prepare them for

The UK government has rejected a total ban on parents smacking children. 'Mild' smacking is allowed under the law. Banned is anything which causes bruising, scratches, reddening of the skin, mental harm or uses an implement.

that? If not, let me suggest this: the goal of parents is to prepare their children to live as mature, independent, productive adults who have a firm moral and spiritual capacity, are capable of loving and being loved and will leave the world a better place for having lived.

Sounds ambitious, doesn't it? What it really boils down to is that, from the day we bring them home from hospital to the day they leave to set up their own home, our goal is to prepare them for successful, independent living. Discipline is a process that takes time.

How can we reach that goal? By giving our children a good example to follow and guiding them carefully as they practise and learn during the period we call growing up. It may not be easy, but it shouldn't be all toil and trouble either! It's an adventure. It's a privilege. It's a gift.

Apprenticed for life

Do you remember when you first 'helped' your mother bake? Perhaps she guided your hand as you measured the flour or showed you how to put the batter in the pan. As you grew older, she left you to do more and more of it yourself. She'd be there to remind you if you forgot an ingredient or to help if you had a problem. Later, she'd let you do it yourself, just checking once in a while to see how it was going. That's still how many young people learn baking, car repairs and other skills today. It's a process of apprenticeship, a term that's not as common today as in the past.

Throughout the Middle Ages and up until the beginning of the Industrial Revolution, the apprenticeship system was the usual way most young people learned. A young person might be apprenticed to a baker, cobbler or other tradesman. By watching, listening and practising under adult guidance, he gradually learned the skills needed to become a responsible, independent adult.

I doubt if the apprenticeship was always a happy time. The young person would have made mistakes and lost his patience now and then, I'm sure. So did his master. But, in spite of problems, it was largely a positive process with a positive outcome.

When I was growing up on my parents' dairy farm, I learned to do the farm chores by working right alongside my dad. At milking time and in the fields, he saw that I learned to do my tasks correctly and to see them through to completion. Those qualities were important to the success of the farm and he knew they would be important to me throughout my adult life. I learned to be 'disciplined' the way most children did through much of history: by observing and working alongside my parents.

We may not be teaching our children vocational skills today, but our children are under our 'apprenticeship' to learn how to live. They watch, listen and practise. We instruct, demonstrate, guide, support and protect. They don't copy our workmanship; they copy our lives.

The question wise parents constantly ask themselves is, 'How can I perform in a competent, mature manner so that I'll be happy when my kids copy me?' Parents in strong families focus on perfecting their own behaviour as much as on perfecting their child's.

Discipling our children

In spiritual terms, we call this process 'discipleship'. The words 'disciple' and 'discipline' come from the same root word meaning 'instruction' or 'teaching'. Disciplining our children involves both patiently teaching them what to believe and how to behave and also demonstrating or modelling responsible behaviour. It means guiding them as they practise making choices, fail, learn from the consequences and try again – all the while giving them the unfailing love and care they need and deserve from us.

As families with faith, what we are aiming for is the kind of home where the parents' faith values are evident in everything and as vital to them as the air they breathe, the water they drink and the food they eat. Values are as important in the daily activities of work and play as they are in moments of crucial decisions.

Does that mean parents have to be perfect? Hardly. We know too well that's not possible. But what really matters to our children, especially our teens, is not that we're perfect but that we're 'real': people who 'walk the talk', admit their failures and keep on trying.

The life of faith, like life in general, is not all success. So, as we disciple our children spiritually, we must let them see our struggles and failures. That way, they can learn the invaluable lesson that the best way to deal with failure is, with God's help, to pick yourself up and move on.

Following God's example

Some of us grew up in families where discipline was more about who was the boss than getting prepared for life. Others remember long lists of rules to be obeyed and harsh punishment when they weren't. How can we shake off these negative images and replace them with a positive approach to discipline?

The place to start is with the example of God, our heavenly Father. God's discipline isn't about power – although he's got plenty of that. The goal of God's discipline isn't behaviour control – although some of that is certainly necessary. God's discipline is about moving his children towards maturity; to becoming all they were intended to be. His motivation is his unconditional love for us. So our discipline is motivated by our unconditional love for our children, unaffected by a child's bad behaviour. As one mother observed, 'When your children are acting the worst, that's when they need your love the most.'

God sets limits and boundaries for us, but their purpose is always positive and loving: to teach us how to live. He allows us freedom to make our own choices but, even when we fail, he's ready to forgive us and help us learn from our failures. Following God's example, parents in families with faith focus most on what their children do right, not wrong. In that way, they build up their children so they can become competent in knowing what is right and confident in choosing it.

> No discipline seems pleasant at the time, but painful. Later on, however, it produces a harvest of righteousness and peace for those who have been trained by it.
> *Hebrews 12:11*

Putting it into practice

Now it's time to see how this positive approach to discipline applies to the everyday process of preparing our children for life. Here are ten guidelines to everyday discipline that parents who disciple their children rely on.

1   THINK POSITIVE!
So much in life is affected by the perspective we bring to it. And a positive perspective isn't always easy to maintain, especially when the two-year-old is sick and the four-year-

old is irritable or the 11-year-old is pouting and the teen is whining. But that's exactly when we need to think positive, even though it takes effort and some creativity!

That's the lesson of this humorous story. One day, a pastor received a call from a man in his congregation telling him that the man's brother had died. He asked the pastor to conduct the funeral.

'There's just one request I have, Pastor,' the man said. 'I know my brother didn't lead the greatest life, but he's gone now. It would mean a lot to me if, during your remarks, you'd call him a saint. And to show my appreciation, I'll donate £1000 to your church building fund.'

That put the pastor in a terrible dilemma. The man who had died was a real scoundrel. His life was no model for anyone! But the building fund needed the money. He struggled and agonised over what to do. How could he find a way to call him a saint?

By the day of the funeral, he'd found a creative way to solve his problem. 'We know that John did not lead a perfect life,' the pastor said in the funeral address. 'He certainly made a lot of mistakes. But he sure was a saint compared to his brother.' The pastor got his £1000.

It's a funny story with a good lesson. Sometimes it takes hard work and creativity to be positive about discipline. It helps to keep in mind what we've learned about discipline so far: it's not punishment; it's not primarily about imposing our will on our children, regardless of their needs or feelings. Rather, it's a process of learning and guidance that is based on respect for your child. Disciplining – or discipling – our children means giving them positive guidance in both our words and actions. It is forward-looking and encouraging. Keeping that in mind helps you find the silver lining in even the most difficult discipline situation.

2 BALANCE LOVE WITH LIMITS

Our culture says that 'all you need is love' to solve any problem. That's a sentimental notion that's got wide appeal. But, when it comes to raising children, love is *not* enough to prepare a child well for life. Love needs to be balanced with limits or rules. Real love means we're not only kind but also firm and fair. In fact, we can't have real love for our children without setting reasonable, healthy limits to guide and nurture them.

Any significant setting of limits, any real discipline of any kind, of course, doesn't start until a child is 18–24 months. Before that, what a child needs most is consistent, loving care and attention. As they grow older, setting limits may make your child feel temporarily unloved. But limits are vital to love. They focus it and give it the substance that makes it real and lasting. That's why a positive approach to limits needs to be accompanied by plenty of hugs, encouragement and kindness.

In families with good survival skills, loving parents understand that, however firm they are, they are gentler teachers than our unforgiving world. So they are willing to do whatever it takes to discipline their children today so that life won't discipline them tomorrow. They balance love with limits.

3 OBSERVE THE 'TWO EARS, ONE MOUTH' RULE

There's an old saying that 'God gave us two ears and one mouth so we could listen twice as much as we speak'. Listening is always one of the most valuable things we can do for another person – and that includes our children of any age. A child's communications should be received as a gift – with tact and gratitude – even when it's not what we had hoped for! Listening when our children talk makes them feel really cared for and important! And it makes sense that children can talk more if parents listen more.

When he was little, our younger son would often come into the house upset or angry over a fight with his friends. Since he was still learning how to get along with others, my wife and I wanted to take advantage of those 'teachable' moments. We quickly learned that if our first reaction was, 'What did you expect? That wasn't a very kind thing to do,' or a similar unsympathetic remark, we only made him more upset and unwilling to listen to us at all. The teachable moment was lost!

When we listen to our children's points of view, they're more likely to feel that we're on their side. Then, they'll be more willing to listen to us. My wife and I learned that it wasn't until we'd listened and been appropriately supportive and sympathetic to our son that he was willing to listen to our advice and correction.

If a child's every attempt to share a problem or frustration is interrupted with, 'But why didn't you do it right the first time?' or 'Haven't I told you before how foolish that is?', soon there won't be any more sharing of confidences! Parents in families with good survival skills know the value of not criticising their children's beliefs and opinions too quickly or harshly. Dacey and Packer write, in their book *The Nurturing Parent*, 'Nothing shuts up a kid faster than an adult who tramples his ideas. Would you reveal your hopes and concerns to someone who consistently told you what was wrong with them?'

When they need to help their children learn a better way, wise parents first look for something to affirm about their child's opinion or values and then calmly say something like, 'Have you thought about it this way?' That helps keep communications open!

Some good advice for parents is found in the ancient wisdom of the book of Proverbs: 'He who answers before listening – that is his folly and his shame,' says Proverbs 18:13. Listen as long as you can. Then, when you do speak, you'll speak with more understanding and ability. But first, listen.

Good listening, like most other important things in family life, requires being available. As children become teens, they tend to confide more in friends, so being available to listen when they want to talk is crucial. In our house, we noticed the best talking opportunity was often in those few minutes when the kids came in the door after school – after the trip to the refrigerator, of course! – or at bedtime.

As a teen, our older son often dropped by our bedroom to talk late in the evening. So sometimes we purposely stayed awake, expecting him to come by to talk. And we were always ready to listen when he did!

With young children, bedtime is often a time of special closeness. They're ready and eager to talk about their experiences and feelings. Yes, this can be a stalling tactic, but not always. The youngest children are less able to organise their thoughts, so it often takes them longer to express them in a way we parents can understand. That requires not just listening, but listening patiently. Sometimes the matter isn't that urgent – except to a three-year-old! Sometimes we really are too busy to listen. At those times, you can still say, 'Let's talk about this at the dinner table' or 'We'll come back to that when I've finished this.' Patient, loving listening builds a bond of intimacy that enables parents to both know their children and successfully disciple them.

4   GIVE THEM SOMETHING TO LIVE UP TO – BUT BE REALISTIC!
As my sons and I stood at my father's graveside after his funeral, we recalled the many kind words people had said about him during the service. They were words such as 'integrity' and 'faithfulness' and 'service'. 'Your grandfather left us quite a standard to live up to,' I told my sons. And we

all wanted to do that.

Educators have known it for years. Children live up (or down) to the expectations we have for them and the standards we set for them. So parents in families with good survival skills keep both expectations and standards high. Average isn't enough for them. After all, if they don't expect the best from their children, who will?

As we've already seen, if we want our children to do their best – in manners, morals or achievements – we must set the example, practising what we preach. But our expectations must also be realistic. If you expect a toddler never to play with her food or a four-year-old never to walk mud into the house, you'll surely be disappointed! If you expect your teen to keep a neat room and enjoy doing chores, you'll be disappointed. It's important to liberally sprinkle your high expectations for your children with a healthy dose of realism. Expect the best – but not beyond the realistic limits of their capability.

Given that our children won't always meet our standards and expectations, how do we help their 'best' get better and better? Catch them doing good! Whenever your child wipes off his shoes before coming in the house, remembers to feed his guinea pig unasked, keeps her room neat or lets you know where she's going when she leaves the house, a wise mum or dad is sure to offer praise. They know that praise encourages similar good behaviour in the future.

Praise

In all our dealings with our children – of any age – praise is a more effective motivator than criticism. Wise parents focus on what their children do right, not wrong. They praise it; they reinforce it. 'Thank you for helping lay the table' is much more effective in encouraging a child to repeat her good behaviour than, 'Well, it's about time you remembered!'

'You're doing much better at putting your toys away,' will more effectively encourage a child to keep trying than, 'What's the matter with you! Haven't I told you dozens of times?'

Unfortunately, most of what children hear from adults today is negative; it centres on their problems and failures. We're quick with criticism, slow with praise. Psychologist James Windell says, 'If you only point out ways in which kids fall short of expectations, failure becomes a self-fulfilling prophecy.' How much better it would be if children heard more positive reminders that, despite their failures, they are moving in the right direction.

'Children will be children' – and that means they sometimes fail to meet even the most realistic expectations. When that happens, wise parents don't dwell on their children's past mistakes but encourage their children to do better in the future. They know that children who are encouraged and trusted are motivated to behave responsibly.

Often it takes a real effort to remain reasonable when our children fail. But parents in strong families give their children this positive message: 'We believe in you. We know you can do it. We know you'll do better next time. We're on your side.' This confidence will help kids through times of discouragement when they really want to give up on a task or give in to temptation.

Children need models, not critics. Critics are all around them. But loving, consistent models are rare. 'Train up a child in the way he should go – and walk that way yourself once in a while' is the way one person humorously put it. In families with good survival skills, parents act as models for their children, not critics. They give them something to live up to!

5   BE A 'YES PARENT'

Dr James Dobson makes a persuasive case for being a 'yes parent'. This is how he puts it: 'No, you can't go out. No, you can't have a cookie. No, you can't use the telephone. And no, you can't go to Susie's house. No, no, no, no. How many times each day do we use that small but powerful word with our children? As parents we could say yes to most routine requests made by our kids. But we often choose, almost automatically, to respond in the negative. Why? Because we don't want to take the time to stop and think about the consequences; because the activity would cause us more work or physical effort; because there might be danger in the request; and because we know our children ask a thousand favours every day, and it's just more convenient to refuse them all.'

Dobson goes on to advise parents not to 'fall into the habit of turning down reasonable requests from our kids. There are so many nos in life that we should say yes whenever we can.' And how does constantly saying 'no' make you look to your child? Do they see you as an overruling judge? A demanding boss? Or do they think of you as a loving parent who is fair and just? One way to build a healthy relationship is to say 'yes', unless there is a very good reason to do otherwise.

Sometimes, of course, there are very good reasons for saying 'no'. A three-year-old doesn't understand limitations of cost or safety. Sometimes, we just want to protect our child from getting hurt or being disappointed – especially when we know we'll be the one to have to pick up the pieces. Sometimes, 'no' really is for a child's own good.

> Fathers, do not exasperate your children; instead, bring them up in the training and instruction of the Lord.
>
> *Ephesians 6:4*

But, in general, Dobson's advice is sound. Here's the rule I try to follow in my family: 'Say *yes unless*, not *no until*. Try to say 'yes' to your child's requests unless there's a good reason *not* to, rather than saying 'no' until they can convince you otherwise. This approach is beneficial to children of all ages and helps minimise confrontations, power struggles, whining and other sorts of problems. It helps make discipline – and family life in general – a lot more positive.

When my younger son was in primary school, his idea of a good Friday night was to have a friend sleep over. And he soon wanted to have a sleepover every weekend! Inevitably, he and his friend would laugh loudly, wrestle wildly and finally go to sleep. Then, they'd start all over again early Saturday morning while my wife and I tried to enjoy our one day to sleep late. It wasn't long before I started saying 'no' to all requests for a Friday night sleepover.

He and I had some heated 'discussions' over this. Being with his friends really was important to my son and their noise was really just a minor inconvenience to me. I really did want to find a way to say 'yes' to his requests. So we arrived at a simple and satisfactory compromise. Overnights could be allowed every other weekend. That seemed fair to us both. Then, I was able to say 'yes' to his sleepover requests.

When we're constantly saying 'no' to our children, no matter what their age or request, parenting becomes an endless series of confrontations and arguments.
- 'Why can't I?'
- 'Because I said so!'
- 'You can't stop me!'
- 'You'd better watch yourself, young man!'

Teens always want more freedom than most parents are comfortable giving. There's a danger of constant friction. So saying 'yes' unless there's a good reason not to is especially helpful with teens. On his graduation from high school, my son wanted to go with friends on a class trip to Mexico. I discovered, however, that the travel agency assumed no responsibility for supervising the class while in Mexico and warned that underage drinking laws were not enforced. So I said 'no' to my son. He wasn't pleased but accepted it surprisingly well. I think it was because he knew I always tried to say 'yes' – so when I said 'no' it was really necessary.

When we're constantly frustrating our children by saying 'no', discipline becomes an exercise in control – how to keep the lid on – rather than discipling. Power struggles and a generally negative atmosphere quickly take over the family.

6   TACKLE POWER STRUGGLES

When your toddler insists on running into the street, you've got to assert control. Her life is at stake. When your teen insists on abusing himself with drugs or alcohol, you've got to assert control. His life is at stake. You have to know when to take control and then do it! Power struggles aren't always avoidable, but they're always regrettable.

And many times power struggles can be avoided. At one of my parenting seminars, a frustrated mother told me of her four-year-old daughter who just wouldn't stay in her room and go to sleep after she turned the lights out. 'I put her to bed, but she keeps coming out of her room and saying she isn't sleepy. I've tried putting her back in the room and threatening her with a spanking but nothing seems to work.'

The mother seemed surprised when I suggested to her that maybe her daughter really *wasn't* tired. 'What does she like most about bedtime?' I asked. 'She likes reading,' she replied.

So I suggested that the child be allowed to stay in her bed with the light on and read until she was ready to fall asleep. But, if she got out of bed, the lights went out and the books were put away. I was pretty sure that, when she got tired enough, she'd fall asleep. That way, her mother could move on to her other evening responsibilities and the daughter could go to sleep when she was tired. Left by herself, with no distractions or stimulation, that's what would happen, I was sure. If it worked, there'd be no more power struggles.

During the seminar, the mother said she was ready to try locking the girl in her room or spanking her repeatedly each evening until she stayed in bed. Those strategies might have 'worked' in the sense of the mother 'winning', but at what cost? The trouble with power struggles is that there are no winners, only losers.

Any parents can 'win' a struggle with their child if they are determined enough. But no child, from toddler to teen, benefits from always being a 'loser'. It eats away at their self-esteem. It builds up frustration, anger and resentment. When family life becomes a series of unending power struggles between parents who always say 'no' and children who need to feel some bit of independence and control over their lives or who want some recognition of their needs and wishes, everybody loses. Parents lose the respect of their children and the joy of parenting. Children lose self-respect and the benefit of learning by doing under the guidance and protection of their parents.

As long as parents are simply trying to 'win', they're trying to make losers out of their children. But the better goal is 'to win children over', not to 'win over children'. By our unconditional love and respect for our children, we strive to win them over to the mature, responsible manner of living that we're teaching and modelling for them. Winning over children through constant power struggles that 'show who's the boss' undermines discipling. And, in the long run, it simply won't work.

7 GIVE CHOICES AND ALTERNATIVES
Being a 'yes' parent not only means saying 'yes' whenever possible, but giving choices and acceptable alternatives

when 'no' is clearly called for.

I learned that lesson with my foster daughter. Antoinette was abandoned by her mother on our pastor's doorstep at the age of four. We took her in and made her a part of our family for five years, until her mother requested and regained legal custody. It was amazing how, at four years old, she seemed to know how to ask for just the wrong thing at just the wrong time! I was constantly saying 'no' to her and neither of us was enjoying each other very much.

I shared my frustration with another parent one day and he suggested I not just say 'no' but, whenever possible, tell her that there was something she *could* do. He called it a 'qualified no' and suggested I say something like, 'You can't do that right now, but how about doing this or that?' I gave her a choice of alternatives acceptable to me and avoided the 'n' word whenever I could. Sometimes, all it takes is a choice to satisfy a child and avoid an unnecessary power struggle.

It's wise to use alternatives to 'no' whenever possible. For example, instead of simply saying to your child, 'No, you can't splash in the water in the sink,' you might be able to say, 'Let's play in the water at bathtime. That's the best place to play in the water.' Or, when a child is asking to play in the garden, 'This isn't a good time to go outside, but what else would be fun to do right now?' Or, when your teen wants to go to an 'adult' movie: 'That's not an acceptable movie to go to. But, if you choose a better one, I'll be glad to take you.'

'Yes parents' try to state limits in a positive way. Often that makes the rules more palatable to a child and teaches not only what isn't allowed but, equally importantly, what is the preferred behaviour. So instead of, 'No, don't interrupt when I'm speaking', you might say, 'It's polite to wait until I've finished talking before you talk. If you stand there quietly, I'll know you want to talk to me.' Or, 'Let's make sure all your toys are in their box before you go to bed', instead of, 'Don't leave your toys in a mess on the floor every night.' Or, 'If you put your clothes in the basket by Friday night, I'll see that they're washed,' rather than, 'If you leave your clothes lying around, they'll never get washed!'

And your 'no' loses its effectiveness if it's overused, anyway. Either your children stop listening or you can't carry through every time you say 'no' and they stop believing you. Better to save your 'no' for a time when you really need it. Because 'yes parents' say 'yes' whenever possible, their children trust that a 'no' must really be necessary and their parents really do mean it. Then they can accept it much more readily.

8   GIVE TEENS APPROPRIATE RESPONSIBILITY

Teens rightly ask for and need to take increasing responsibility for their lives. So families with good survival skills give teens more and more responsibility as they mature and rely increasingly on discussion, negotiation and compromise to set limits.

One parent decided her teenage children would have no bedtime rules. Her children go to sleep when they're tired. 'If they fall asleep in school, then we have a problem, which we'll deal with. But they aren't dumb; they know that, if they fall asleep during the day, it's because they're staying up too late at night. So they'll give me a sheepish grin and decide to go to bed earlier.'

This same mother had an 11pm curfew for her teenage daughter for a while, but regularly there seemed to be good reasons (school activities, trips with other families, for example) for her coming in later. So the family dropped the arbitrary rule and decided to discuss each situation separately to arrive at a reasonable time for the daughter to be home.

When my older son was 16, I didn't want to set a firm

curfew for him for similar reasons. Events such as cinema showings or school functions had different ending times, meaning we'd have to negotiate a specific time to be home, anyway. Often, as he was getting ready to leave, I'd ask him, 'When do you plan to be home?' More often than not, I got an acceptable answer and said, 'Fine. I'll expect to see you then. If you have a problem, just give me a call.' That way, *he* took responsibility for setting his own curfew and observing it. If his suggested arrival time wasn't satisfactory, we'd negotiate one that was.

A similar approach works well with disputes. If your teen wants to do something of which you don't approve, discussion and negotiation can be very positive. You can share your concerns with your teen (an education for them!) and ask them what suggestions they have for dealing with them. Often, they come up with acceptable suggestions or compromises. When they do, it's no longer *your* rules that have bound them, but *their* agreed solutions.

'Yes parents' understand that negotiation and compromise help children to learn important skills of living and to feel respected at the same time. Whether the issue is clothing, curfews, driving or dating, wise parents of teens know that negotiation and compromise is a necessary tool. They pick their battles carefully but, because they love their children, they don't shrink from the really important ones. Where serious issues of morality, legality, health and safety are concerned, even a 'yes parent' will firmly say 'no'. They balance their unconditional love with clear limits.

9   LET THEM PRACTISE DECISION-MAKING

There's an old story about a tourist who approached a cab driver in New York for directions. The man wanted to attend a concert at Carnegie Hall. 'Excuse me, sir,' he said to the cab driver. 'How do you get to Carnegie Hall?' The cab driver replied, 'That's easy, friend. Practise, practise, practise!'

Learning to do anything well usually requires practice. Learning to live successfully as an adult is no exception. But learning to live is different from learning to play the violin or flute. For an adult, daily life is a series of choices: some big, some small. The skill of making good choices – big or small – is learned through practice. We make choices, see the consequences, learn from our failures and successes and move ahead to the next one.

God's plan for parents is that they 'work themselves out of a job' by preparing their children for responsible, independent living. Children get better at things they practise. They must be given responsibility if they are to become responsible and they must make their own decisions if they are to learn to have good judgement. So it's wise to allow your children to practise making age-appropriate choices early in life and continue that until your children leave home.

When children are given appropriate choices, they learn an important lesson: 'I'm responsible for choosing and for what happens as a result. So I'd better choose carefully.' Such choices are not a threat to a parent's authority. After all, who gave the child the choices?

At first the choices are very simple. You might allow your three-year-old to decide which of two shirts to wear today or which of two or three friends to invite over to play for the afternoon. By ten or 11, the same child may be allowed to choose when to do homework (after school or after dinner) and have wider freedom over what to wear to school.

One of the advantages of giving a child appropriate choices is that it puts responsibility right where it belongs: on the child. 'I'm sorry about your friend wanting to come over tonight, but you did chose to do your homework after dinner. Maybe she can come over tomorrow.' There's less need for nagging. After all, whose choice was it to do homework after dinner?

As children progress through the teen years, their choices grow more serious. By the mid-teens, children generally choose their own friends – whether we like them or not! They begin to demand choices about where they go, what they do, when and with whom. They make academic and vocational choices, as well as choices about personal conduct, values and faith.

How do parents 'disciple' or discipline children in the mid to late teen years? Most often, they do it by taking on the role of a 'coach' or 'mentor'. They give their children less direction and provide more advice and encouragement – still, whenever necessary, setting clear limits. Most importantly, successful discipling parents give their teens more and more freedom to practise making many everyday choices. In other words, their parents trust them.

'I'll trust you until...'

When my older son was about 15, I intentionally said to another adult while my son was listening: 'I don't worry about him. I'll trust him until he gives me reason not to.' That became my rule with my son during his teenage years: 'I'll trust you until you give me reason not to.' I gave him trust to live up to. It was a gift. He didn't have to earn it. It was his until he lost it. He never did.

Nothing is more important to our children, especially our teens, than feeling that we trust them (in age-appropriate situations). And nothing is more crucial to their success in learning to make wise choices than our trust. Sometimes we're not sure our children are really trustworthy. Giving them the trust they need can be pretty scary! But our trust gives them something to live up to as they make their own choices.

In strong families, parents trust their children's judgement because they've modelled for their children how to make good decisions. They trust their morals because they've raised them in a moral environment. And they've helped them practise making good choices by letting them make decisions and assume responsibility as they mature. That's how discipling or apprenticeship works.

Does trusting our children with choices mean expecting they'll never make mistakes? Of course not. After all, 'practice makes perfect'. But, as they keep practising, they'll learn from their mistakes.

10 LET THEM LEARN FROM 'THE SCHOOL OF HARD KNOCKS'
In the Bible story about the lost son (Luke 15:11–32) to which we've already referred in chapter 7, there's no doubt that the father dearly loved his two sons. The younger asked his father for his share of the family inheritance because he didn't want to wait until his father's death; he wanted to enjoy his share now.

Later events in the story make clear that the son was still immature, and his father surely realised it. He probably foresaw much of the foolish behaviour in which his son engaged and which resulted in his wasting his inheritance. I'm sure that the father advised his son to reconsider his decision.

In the end, however, the father honoured his son's choice. He let him go off on his own and waste his inheritance on what the story describes as 'wild living'. Penniless, the son had to take a job feeding pigs just to survive. Ashamed of his foolishness, he returned home to beg his father to hire him as a servant. That way, he could once again enjoy at least a small bit of comfort and security. He had learned his lesson the hard way. Sometimes that's the best way or even the only way children will learn.

Every child must learn that all actions (and the choices that lead to them) have consequences:

- 'If you don't wear proper clothing in the winter when you go outside to play, you'll be cold and have to stop playing and come in to dress more warmly.'
- 'If you don't eat enough at breakfast, you'll be hungry long before lunch.'
- 'If you're unkind to others, you won't have any friends.'
- 'If you don't do your homework or chores on time, you'll lose the opportunity to do something else.'

When my younger son was 11, I stopped nagging him about wearing a warm coat to school. He was old enough to make his own choice. If he was cold waiting for the bus, he could come back for it if he had time. If not, he'd be cold that day. I was certain he'd learn a valuable lesson from that choice. There'd be no need for me to nag.

When he was 14, I stopped reminding him that it was time for bed. At first, he stayed up too late a few times. But he didn't like being sleepy and irritable in school the next day, so he began to go to bed at about the same time I would have set for him, sometimes even earlier. But I didn't have to set or enforce his bedtime. He chose it. He had made some poor choices about bedtime, suffered the consequences and learned from his (ultimately harmless) mistake. Learning that way was much more effective than if I had simply nagged him to go to bed.

That's another benefit of letting children experience the consequences of their actions. Often they discover their own limits (how much sleep they need, how much time it takes to finish their chores), 'self-correct' and choose their own appropriate limits. That's very 'adult' behaviour and good for any child to learn!

But what if they don't 'self-correct'? What would I have done if my son had gone for two weeks staying up until midnight, repeatedly falling asleep in school and perhaps even getting sick from being overtired? Then it's time to temporarily take back the choice that was given. 'You're falling asleep in school and getting sick from being overtired. I can see that you're not getting enough sleep. Please be in bed by 10pm from now on.' Then, after some appropriate time for your child to learn (perhaps six months or a year), you let them try again. In the end, a child needs to learn to make good choices and gain confidence in their ability to make them. That can only come with practice.

When safety is not an issue, letting children get an education in 'The School of Hard Knocks' is the most effective way to prepare them for life. While they are young, we need to protect them from dangerous choices. But, if we don't let them learn from the consequences of their mistakes when they are young and the consequences are relatively minor, they may have to be taught by reality when they are older and the consequences are much more serious.

I know from experience that this approach to discipline is a lot of work! But in the long run, it pays much greater returns in the lives of our children. In developing self-discipline, as in most areas of life, 'practice makes perfect!'

Keep a sense of humour and a sense of perspective!

I grew up in a family of four children, each two to three years apart. We were just close enough in age to be textbook examples of sibling rivalry – always fighting. At least four times an hour, it seemed, one of us would run to Mom to complain of some terrible injustice perpetrated on us. 'Don't make a criminal offence out of it,' she'd say.

That was my mother's way of telling us to relax and keep things in perspective. Some things can be treated with the neglect they deserve. Every little failure isn't worth nagging or rebuking a child for. There are times when it won't make a whole lot of difference if things aren't done 'just right, right now,' whether it's taking out the rubbish or cleaning up a room.

Children have bad days and bad moods, just like the rest of us. Sometimes the common sense approach is simply to ignore unimportant things, especially sulky faces or whining tones. This not only gives your children space to work on their own relationships but keeps the atmosphere lighter and lets you keep your 'thunder' for things that really matter.

So my wife and I try to live by what we call 'the DBSS Rule': Don't Bother with the Small Stuff. A lot of family strife is over things that aren't important in the long run. And sometimes, when your children have been less than perfect, a little humour can be just what is needed. Laugh a little. Have a funny saying in your family that can trigger a smile when one is desperately needed. When your child whines or complains, try, 'I guess it's just a bad day. I think I'll whine too!'

A word about sibling rivalry

Discussion of discipling inevitably raises the issue of sibling rivalry – the cause of much squabbling and family stress. It's a problem that has existed as long as families have; just think about Joseph's difficult relationship with his brothers! Factors identified as causing dissent between siblings are:
- differences in temperament;
- differences in sex: a boy may resent his sister because he feels she is treated more gently, for example; or a girl may resent not being allowed the freedom her brother is given;
- differences in age: a four- and a seven-year-old will often play happily together, but at ten and 13 they will find it harder to relate to one another;
- position in family: the older child being given res-ponsibilities for the younger, for example.

Unsurprisingly, sibling rivalry is 'normal'. But parental

attitude is important in minimising the battles. Being impartial can be very difficult, especially when children have different personalities and needs. Here are just three pointers towards keeping the peace:

- Don't make comparisons between the siblings; help each to feel appreciated as unique, different.
- Don't dismiss your children's anger or resentment; accept it as genuine and normal and discuss it with them calmly.
- Try to avoid situations that provoke antagonism between siblings, being prepared to intervene early in anything that might be expected to result in confrontation. However, when disputes occur it's sometimes helpful to let them run their course and allow the children to settle things themselves when they can.

No guarantees

When all is said and done, there are no guarantees in life – either that children will have perfect parents or that parents will raise children who become perfect adults. We do our best for 18 years or so, and then our children grow up and move away. They become independent adults. That's what we've worked for. That's God's plan.

As adults, our children make their own choices. Some are good; some are not. But they are their choices, not ours. And, again, there are no guarantees except this: God is faithful. We can trust him. He honours our efforts to be the best parents we can be.

When our children leave home, in one sense we may be done with parenting, but God is not. Long after our children have grown up, God hears our prayers for them. Long after we are no longer there for our children, God is. So we know we can trust our children to God. He loves them even more than we do.

Building survival skills 10: Disciplining is discipling!

Discipline is a hot topic for most parents, and rightly so. But discipling our children *can* be a very positive, exciting process. Evaluate your understanding and application of discipline as discipling in your family, using these questions.

1   How would you describe your understanding of and approach to discipline in your family? Has it changed since reading this chapter? If so, how?

2   'No discipline seems pleasant at the time, but painful. Later on, however, it produces a harvest of righteousness and peace for those who have been trained by it' (Hebrews 12:11). In what ways is your discipline intended to produce 'a harvest of righteousness and peace' in your children? What changes, if any, might you make?

3   How does your personal life and example contribute to (or undermine) your discipline as discipling? In what ways might you strengthen your example?

4   Can you think of specific ways you want to give greater choices and new ways to allow your children to 'practise' independence this week? If so, list them.

5   Which of the ten guidelines to everyday discipline listed in the chapter is (or are) most challenging to you? How might you attempt to grow in those areas?

SURVIVAL SKILL 6

Being supported by the Church

11 Reaching out to build families

WHATEVER ELSE it is, a church is certainly a family: the family of God. Paul talks of 'those who belong to the family of believers' (Galatians 6:10); and about God's 'whole family in heaven and on earth' (Ephesians 3:15). So, as part of a worldwide family, the local church should be a place where everyone finds welcome and support. As we've seen, families greatly need support as they struggle to survive and thrive in the midst of the challenges of maintaining a healthy work/family balance. They need support managing family time, dealing with financial pressures and succeeding in new shapes and sizes.

Increasingly, churches are aware of the struggles of today's families and are offering help and support. In this chapter, we'll look at some of the ways churches are already doing this and point to some new ways that support can be given.

Family-friendly churches?

Do families feel welcome in your church? What makes a church 'family-friendly'? What makes a church a place where single parents, blended families, couples without children, two-parent families with children – in short, families of all different shapes and sizes – feel welcome and supported?

In such a church, families of all kinds must not only feel that their needs are recognised but also, as far as possible, met. For example, the church facilities have wheelchair ramps for families with elderly or disabled members. Families with young children will find facilities that are safe and in good repair, with bright, friendly spaces for young children to play and learn in, and toilets with changing tables for infants. The worship area in the church I attend has a balcony fitted with a high railing so that young children can't easily fall over it. There should also be clear guidelines regarding child protection so children can be safe at all times.

A 'family-friendly' church will have a creative, inspiring children's programme and an active youth ministry for teens (jointly run with another church, if necessary). It will be a church that provides its families opportunities for learning and growing by offering (or paying the attendance costs of) seminars and events for parents, marriage partners, engaged couples, singles, teens and the elderly. Where the church is of a sufficient size, it may also run support groups for lone-parent and blended families, divorce recovery, singles, families with disabled members and perhaps even those with family members in prison.

Recognising the time pressures on families, a family-friendly church will limit the evening meetings when family members are expected to be at church, whether for choir rehearsal, Bible study or a community project. And churches will be aware of scheduling clashes such as service times and sports practices. Some churches might support families by speaking out against events that are scheduled too close to the evening mealtime or on Sunday mornings; or alternatively they might consider changing their service times.

Families in crisis

Families do find themselves in crisis from time to time and a family-friendly church is equipped to provide appropriate support. Families in crisis will be able easily to identify who they can contact for help. Financial aid and other kinds of practical support such as providing meals and respite for care givers may be offered. Appropriate pastoral or crisis counselling is often available from the church staff too. And a truly 'family-friendly' church is always seeking ways to reach out in the name of Christ, in service and support of the families in its immediate neighbourhood – whether they are church members or not.

Of course, not every church can provide every means of support I've mentioned. But every church can do something – and many can probably do more than they are doing right now. If it sees a need and can't meet it alone, then that's the time to join with other churches in the area to tackle the issue. Many times, a group of churches working together can provide measures of support which no church alone can offer.

Supporting families in need

Many, if not most, congregations have families in need among them or on their doorstep. They may be hidden because they are too embarrassed to share their need, and the need may only be temporary, such as the need for transitional housing or financial need caused by temporary unemployment.

The deacons in one church I know provide families who are struggling financially with vouchers for a local supermarket. They also provide emergency funds for rent and utility payments, especially in the winter.

At the church where I worship, the deacons periodically appeal to the congregation for funds to meet special needs in the community. Names of those in need are rarely mentioned but the need is clearly specified. Another church takes up a special offering each month specifically for the use of the church council in meeting the needs of families in crisis. Some churches operate a food parcel scheme for local families in need or, by bulk buying, operate a non-profit-making shop which sells basic food cupboard items at cost.

The Willow Creek Community Church in suburban Chicago, one of the largest churches in the US, sponsors a food store as part of its Community Care Centre. Food is available to needy individuals and families six days a week. Part of the food distributed comes from the church's Giving Garden Programme. In 2005, over 1000 kilos of vegetables were donated from the gardens of church members. The church also has a small garden on its own property which is tended by volunteer church members. Many churches could begin a smaller, but no less effective, version of a Giving Garden to support their own or a community food project.

Care needs

Many children in needy areas face two daily challenges: getting regular meals and having a safe place to be after school before their parents arrive home from work. Some children are sent to school each day with little or no breakfast and, as research recognises, the lack of a good breakfast negatively effects their ability to learn.

Churches in both the UK and the US are helping children meet those urgent needs. Some churches now sponsor a breakfast club for children before school for one or several days a week. The children have a safe place to be for up to an hour before school while receiving a nutritious breakfast.

In the US, Scripture Union and the Salvation Army have partnered to provide a safe place for children to meet after school while learning about God's love for them. The programme, called PrimeTime, meets in Salvation Army facilities throughout the north-east section of the country and provides children aged six to 11 a safe, inviting place to come for up to two and a half hours after school. The children get a snack, help with homework, learn about the Bible and have a fun activity too. The programme is designed so that it can also be run by individual churches.

Housing help for families

Finding affordable housing is a challenge for many low-income families. Other families need urgent home repairs that they are unable to pay for. Some may have a disabled child or a chronically sick adult and need modifications to their home. Some may simply be elderly or singles who need help with simple jobs such as gardening or minor repairs. Many local churches in the US send work crews on Saturdays to build affordable housing for families through Habitat for Humanity or similar organisations, while others send out teams to help with repairs, modifications and other family housing needs.

Support for marriage and family relationships

This is perhaps the most common area where churches today are supporting families. Many churches throughout the UK sponsor marriage preparation and enrichment classes. Typical of many is the Catholic Diocese of Arundel and Brighton, which has a large Family Life Ministry that aims to

> Carry each other's burdens, and in this way you will fulfil the law of Christ.
> *Galatians 6:2*

build supportive relationships among families in the church and offers extensive marriage preparation, marriage enrichment and parenting classes throughout the year.

There are many other examples, too. The Catholic Diocese of Leeds offers parenting courses at churches throughout the area. Their family life courses offer help in planning and budgeting family finances – as we saw in chapter 5, a real necessity for survival for single-parent families. The Anglican Diocese of Worcester combines parenting and family support by providing a ministry to fathers in prison to help them learn to bond with their children and maintain that bond while locked away.

Even small churches can offer marriage preparation and enrichment classes and parenting seminars through the many that are available on video. Marriage mentoring is also gaining popularity. Programmes such as Marriage Savers in the US train mature couples within the congregation to be mentors to help other couples prepare for a lifelong marriage, strengthen existing marriages and restore troubled ones.

Support groups

Often, new mothers feel isolated and without a supportive network to provide encouragement and emotional support. For them, the Oxford Anglican Diocese offers a First Time Mums project sponsored by the Mothers' Union. Many other churches provide a room, refreshments and childcare for a local parents' group to meet weekly for a programme of supportive, practical talks or Bible study and prayer.

Divorce recovery workshops and support groups are not new, but are a continuing need that churches can meet. Such programmes not only signal that the church welcomes divorced people, but provide emotional and practical support for them as they attempt to recover and grow, spiritually and emotionally.

Dealing with all the daily pressures and challenges of parenting is enough to wear down even the strongest parent. That's why support groups can be such a fruitful ministry to parents – parents of teens, parents of toddlers, parents of disabled children, parents caring for their own parents, single parents or parents in blended families. All it takes is for a church to identify a few families in the congregation or the neighbourhood who share a similar challenge and invite them to meet together for fellowship and mutual support! A church that does that is well on the road to being family-friendly.

Support for unemployed parents

Being unemployed puts significant strains on families and sometimes just a little encouragement and help towards re-employment is all that's needed to get a family back on its feet, surviving and thriving. One church I know sponsors a weekly support group for people who have lost their job, offering counselling on how and where to find a new one.

Larger churches may be able to do what the Willow Creek Community Church does: they sponsor a Careers Ministry that helps unemployed people find work and even provides a website for employers to post notices of available jobs and where job seekers can search for a position. A group of churches in the Albany area of New York state joined together to give a grant to a non-profit organisation called Second Blessing. Second Blessing trains people (primarily women, often single mums) to put on home parties, enabling them to earn an income through commission on sales.

Support for single parents

We've already seen some of the special challenges that lone parents face. Churches are increasingly stepping up to support single mums and dads in creative ways that really make a difference. The mere fact that a church has a recognised single-parent ministry signals to them that they are welcome in the church, that their needs are recognised, that they are not second class citizens in God's kingdom.

Again, the Willow Creek Community Church in suburban Chicago models an exceptional ministry to lone parents. It offers a teaching programme emphasising spiritual growth and provides a self-help network. There are social events as well as seminars on parenting and practical topics like financial skills. While the parents are attending, their children attend their own programme called Champions, where they have fun, a light meal and learn about God's love. The ministry also sponsors family events for single-parent families, such as visits to local attractions, camping and roller-skating.

One of the challenges facing lone parents when they want to get out for a social event – even just a cup of coffee with a friend – is the need for childcare. Some churches are now offering free childcare one night a month to single parents in their fellowship. It might be offered at a set time with the children being minded at the church or older teens may be dispatched to mind children in their own home. And, of course, any family-friendly church offers childcare at all church meetings!

There's so much more!

In chapter 5, when we discussed lone-parent and blended families, we saw something of the pain that children feel when their parents separate or divorce. Willow Creek Church provides a ministry called Oasis to children up to 18 years of age going through their parent's marriage problems, separation or divorce. The programme meets for two hours weekly for 30 weeks of the year, coinciding with divorce recovery or marriage workshops. Children who attend are loved, affirmed and have a teaching time (dealing with topics such as trust, anger and forgiveness) and fun activities.

Not every church can offer such extensive programmes, but many churches could offer a weekly fun and fellowship night for single-parent families. It wouldn't need to be expensive or elaborate but it would be an affirming, welcoming ministry that would speak clearly of God's love for these families as expressed through the larger family of the church.

One of the increasingly common ways churches are offering Christian service to lone parents, especially women, is through a transport ministry. In my area and around the country, churches whose members include car mechanics or men with skills in minor car repairs offer help such as oil changes, engine tuning and servicing to single mothers in the fellowship and the community. Some larger churches receive donated cars and give them to parents who need reliable transportation in order to manage their jobs.

Here again, Willow Creek Church has established a model for such a ministry. Their CARS ministry (Christian Auto Repairmen Serving) provides mechanical repairs and services and reconditions donated vehicles which are provided to people in need, including single parents. But the benefits don't flow just to the recipients of the services. The volunteer repairmen grow relationally and spiritually as they use their gifts to serve people with transportation needs. Of course, this is an ambitious programme for most individual churches to undertake, but a group of churches could pool the mechanical skills of their members to offer this type of ministry to families throughout the community.

Churches and families need each other

Churches not only *are* families, but they also *need* families in order to grow and to reflect the fullness of God's kingdom. And families need churches in order to mature in their faith, survive the pressures and meet the challenges all around them. Whatever a church can do in Christ's name to support families is really worthwhile – no matter how big or small.

The way to begin is by identifying obvious needs of families in your church and neighbourhood. Then assess the gifts, abilities and other resources available in your church and community to meet those needs. Pray with other people who are similarly concerned and ask God to show you the one or two ways of supporting families that are best for your church. Then you're ready to begin.

What if you identify a significant need to support families which seems totally beyond the capability of one church? Perhaps some church members feel a real calling to provide it but the task seems overwhelming. That's when it's time to think 'partnership'. Link up and serve through your city or neighbourhood mission, the local food co-operative, women's shelter or the Salvation Army. Contact an umbrella organisation such as your local diocese or Churches Together for Families (CTF) and work with and through them.

Churches that support families not only perform a vital service to society but offers church members a concrete way to live out their faith by serving others in the name of Christ. As they do, churches, families and the larger society are all greatly blessed.

Building survival skills 11: Reaching out to build families

Families today need plenty of support. What better place for it to come from than the Church, the 'family of families'? Spend some time now assessing how you and your church can support families.

1 In what ways is your church family-friendly? In what ways could it be more so?

2 'Carry each other's burdens and in this way you will fulfil the law of Christ' (Galatians 6:2). How does your church practise this with regard to families both in and outside the fellowship? What additional ways of carrying one another's burdens would you like to see your church practise in regard to families?

3 Identify some of the outstanding unmet needs of families in your church and its neighbourhood.

4 Identify any potential resources (people, skills, funding, etc) in your church that could be used to meet those needs. How could you engage them in that mission?

5 Are there other churches, ministries or umbrella organisations with which volunteers from your church could partner in supporting families? List them here.

6 What should be the first step your church should take in growing its support for families? What, specifically, can you and your family do to get started?

And, in conclusion...

IF YOU'RE already a parent, you knew before you ever picked up this book that good parenting doesn't come easy. You can't go to college and get a degree in parenting. We all learn the same way – by trial and error. And we all experience plenty of both.

Just as we recognise that there are no perfect parents, neither are there perfect children. We can't programme our children like computers to turn out just the way we want. But that shouldn't and needn't stop us parents from drawing deep joy and many rewards from this great gift of God that we call being a parent.

That's been the aim of this book; to demonstrate that in the midst of all the pressures and forces acting against families with faith, there are some simple survival skills that enable them to survive and thrive; to really enjoy being a family.

Along the way, we've learned important lessons from the experience of many other families of faith and those that support them. We've learned how families just like ours master their time to stay connected and grow together when there seems hardly enough time just to get by. We've seen how families today are gradually gaining the upper hand in beating back the job culture, and maintaining a better balance between the competing demands of work and family life.

There are so many ways that families of faith creatively enjoy each other, celebrate being a family and have fun together – no matter whether they're traditional two-parent families, single-parent families or blended families. And we've drawn from their hard-learned lessons on a positive approach to discipline. Why not just rely totally on the experts? Don't they know best? Not really. *You* are the expert with your child. You know the values you want to pass on to your child. God, who gave our children to us, also gave us both the responsibility and the resources to be their parents. That's why it's just as important to listen to what other parents have learned as to look to experts.

Hopefully, one lesson that's become clear is that, whatever the pressures or challenges, no parent needs to be alone – not even single parents. Every family of faith has a great pool of resources available in the support of their bigger family – the Church – and in partnership with their heavenly 'parent', God the Father.

In a sense, I've saved the best for last, because drawing on the resources of our faith and our faith community is the most foundational of all survival skills for families of faith. Let me rephrase a key spiritual principle mentioned earlier: *As you deepen your personal discipleship (your growing personal relationship to God), you strengthen your family.* Keep in tune with your faith community and keep close to God. Grow your faith and that of your family. As you do, you'll grow in the wisdom and confidence needed for your family to survive and thrive! And, in fact, I'm confident that they will!

Source notes

In researching and writing this book I drew on the wisdom of a great many other books, articles and websites – many more than can easily be mentioned. The most significant are listed here.

Websites

www.surestart.gov.uk is a UK government programme aiming to bring together early education, childcare, health and family support.

www.home-start.org.uk is a UK charity running a network of 12,000 trained parent volunteers who offer support to struggling families with problems such as post-natal depression, disability and social isolation.

Surviving the time crunch and staying connected

R Taylor, *Britain's World of Work: Myths and Realities* (ERSC Future of Work Programme) based on survey work (*Working in Britain in the Year 2000*) by the Policy Study Institute and The London School of Economics; CIPD, 2001, cited in *Balancing Work and Family Life: Enhancing Choice and Support of Parents*, Department of Trade and Industry report, 2003.

Warde, Olsen, et al, *Time Use Surveys and the Changing Organisation of Everyday Life in the UK: 1975–2000*, Economic and Social Research Council, July, 2004.

Listening 2004 report issued by The Catholic Bishops of England and Wales.

Dolores Curran, *Traits of a Healthy Family,* Winston Press, 1983.

Nick Stinnett and John DeFrain, *Secrets of Strong Families,* Berkeley Books, 1986.

www.bbc.co.uk/parenting

www.keeptimeforchildren.org.uk

Creating and enjoying the family Sabbath

Marva J Dawn, *Keeping the Sabbath Wholly,* Eerdmans, 1989.

Lynne Baab, *Sabbath Keeping: Finding Freedom in the Rhythms of Rest*, InterVarsity Press, 2005.

Don Postema, *Catch Your Breath: God's Invitation to Sabbath Rest*, CRC Publications, 1997.

Balancing work and family

Balancing Work and Family Life: Enhancing Choice and Support for Parents, Department of Trade and Industry report, January 2003.

Working Time – Widening the Debate: A Preliminary Consultation on Long Hours Working in the UK and the Application and Operation of the Working Time Opt Out, Department of Trade and Industry report, June 2004.

Richard Patterson, Jr, *Brand-Name Kids: The Loss of Childhood in America,* Fleming Revell, 1988.

Kyle D Pruett, *The Nurturing Father: Journey Toward the Complete Man,* Warner Books, 1987.

www.flexibility.co.uk/flexwork/time/time-options.htm

www.workingmother.com

www.workingfamilies.org.uk

Growing a happy marriage

O R Johnson, *Who Needs The Family?* InterVarsity Press, 1979.

Nick Stinnett and John DeFrain, *Secrets of Strong Families*, Berkeley Books, 1986.

Paul Stephens, *Marriage Spirituality,* InterVarsity Press, 1989.

Lee Strobel and Leslie Strobel, *Surviving a Spiritual Mismatch in Marriage*, Zondervan, 2002.

Listening 2004 report issued by The Catholic Bishops of England and Wales.

Ronald W Pierce and Rebecca Merrill Groothuis, *Discovering Biblical Equality: Complementarity Without Hierarchy*, InterVarsity Press, 2004.

Surviving and thriving in single-parent and blended families

Kevin Lehman, *Single Parenting that Works,* Tyndale House Publishers, 2006.

Jim Smoke, *Seven Keys to a Healthy Blended Family,* Harvest House Publishers, 2004.

Joann and Seth Webster, *Can Step Families Be Done Right?* Creation House, 2001.

Jan Prior, *Step Families and Resilience: Final Report*, a study by the Ministry of Social Development in New Zealand, 2004.

Fathers 4 Justice: *www.fathers-4-justice.org*

Gingerbread: *www.gingerbread.org.uk*

Single Parents UK: *www.singleparents.org.uk*

StepFamilies UK: *www.stepfamilies.co.uk*

BabyCentre: *www.babycentre.co.uk*

Practical Parent: *www.practicalparent.org.uk*

Equal Parenting Council: *www.equalparenting.org*

Care for the Family: *www.careforthefamily.org.uk*

Parentline Plus: *www.parentlineplus.org.uk*

Blended Families: *www.blendedfamilies.com*

Blended Family Resource Center:
www.blendedfamilyresourcecenter.com

Life in a Blender: *www.lifeinablender.com*

Father's Rights US: *www.fathersrights.com*

Father's Rights, Inc: *www.fathersrightsinc.com*

American Coalition for Fathers and Children: *www.acfa.org*

Successful Stepfamilies: *www.successfulstepfamilies.com*

Building your family's faith in the home

J Otis Ledbetter and Tim Smith, *Family Traditions: Practical, Intentional Ways to Strengthen Your Family Identity,* Chariot Victor Publishing, 1998.

Praying for your children

Stormie Omartian, *The Power of a Praying Parent,* Harvest House Publishers, 1995.

Making family memories: rituals and traditions

Paul Pearsall, *The Power of the Family: Strength, Comfort and Healing,* Doubleday, 1990.

J Otis Ledbetter and Tim Smith: *Family Traditions: Practical, Intentional Ways to Strengthen Your Family Identity,* Chariot Victor Publishing, 1998.

Susan Abel Lieberman, *New Traditions: Redefining Celebrations for Today's Family,* Farrar, Strauss & Giroux, 1991.

David B Batchelder, *All Through the Day, All Through the Year: Family Prayers and Celebrations,* Augsburgh Fortress, 2000.

Meg Cox, *The Book of New Family Traditions,* Running Press, 2003.

Having fun is serious business

Dolores Curran, *Traits of a Healthy Family,* Winston Press, 1983.

Richard Patterson, Jr, *Brand-Name Kids: The Loss of Childhood in America,* Fleming Revell, 1988.

Thinking positive about discipline

Jay Kessler, *Raising Responsible Kids,* Wolgemuth and Hyatt, 1991.

Jack O and Judith K Baliswick, *The Family: A Christian Perspective on the Contemporary Home,* Baker Book House, 1991.

Ray Guarendi with David Eich, *Back to the Family,* Simon and Schuster, 1990.

John S Dacey and Alex J Packer, *The Nurturing Parent,* Simon and Schuster, 1992.

Being supported by the Church

www.willowcreek.org

www.marriagesavers.org

Other useful publications:

Family nights

Family Nights Tool Chest, Victor Books – an excellent series of books by various authors, full of good teaching and including lots of fun activities for the family.

Dean and Grace Merrill, *Together at Home: 100 Proven Ways to Nurture your Children's Faith*, Thomas Nelson, 1996.

David R Veerman, *Serious Fun*, Victor Books, 1995.

Family atmosphere

Robert Lewis, *Real Family Values*, Multnomah, 1995.

Robert E Webber, *The Book of Family Prayer*, Hendrickson, 1996.

David Batchelder, *All Through the Day, All Through the Year: Family Prayers and Celebrations*, Augsburg Fortress 2000.

Dan and Elizabeth Hamilton, *Look Both Ways: Helping Your Children Stay Innocent and Grow Wise*, InterVarsity Press, 1999.

Bible Reading Help for All Ages

Encounter with God

Encounter with God takes you through the OT once, NT twice, in 5 years. Especially helpful for experienced Bible readers.

Discovery

Discovery takes you through major portions of every Bible book in 4 years. Gives you practical help from the Bible.

OneUp

One Up. For youth ages 11-14, covers a large portion of the Bible in 4 years. Includes special features for teens.

SnapShots

Snapshots. For ages 7-10, each day covers a short Bible passage with simple explanations, and activity material.

Cost: $22/yr. (published quarterly). Call SU/USA at 1-800-621-LAMP(5267) or visit www.ScriptureUnion.org to order.